The Fiction Kitchen Trio COOKBOOK

Novel Recipes from Your Favorite Novels

SARAH M. EDEN
SIAN ANN BESSEY
TRACI HUNTER ABRAMSON

Cover image: *Authors* © Melea Nelson 2021

Cover design copyright © 2023 by Covenant Communications, Inc.

Published by Covenant Communications, Inc.
American Fork, Utah

Printed in the United States of America
First Printing: March 2023

32 31 30 29 28 27 26 25 24 23   10 9 8 7 6 5 4 3 2 1

ISBN 978-1-52442-132-8

For Samantha Millburn and Amy
Parker, who continue to believe in us
regardless of our seemingly crazy ideas

Acknowledgments

This cookbook began as a fanciful thought in the middle of the night, and it took a small army of people to turn that original, farfetched notion into a book of recipes from our most-loved characters.

Thank you, Samantha Millburn and Amy Parker, for championing our vision in those early meetings at Covenant. Thank you, Robby Nichols, for giving us the go-ahead, and Margaret Weber and her fabulous design team, for working with us on the cookbook cover and layout. Christina Marcano, we know you usually work with more skilled and elegant models, but you did an incredible job with what you were given. Thank you.

We are grateful to Annie Petersen, our wonderful editor on this project, and Lara Abramson, who went above and beyond to help us proofread and make necessary changes to our recipes. Thanks, also, to our family members and friends who endured weeks of taste-testing as we honed our recipes. It was a daunting task, but we appreciate your willingness to step up to the plate for us.

Finally, but most importantly, thank you to our readers and followers on *The Fiction Kitchen Trio* social media pages. Your love for our characters, enthusiasm for our bake-offs and cook-offs, and requests for our recipes are what made this cookbook a reality. We have taken you into our kitchens, and you feel like friends. We hope you and your families enjoy these recipes for years to come.

Praise for the Fiction Kitchen Trio Cookbook

"*The Fiction Kitchen Trio Cookbook: Novel Recipes from Your Favorite Novels* by Sarah M. Eden, Traci Hunter Abramson, and Sian Ann Bessey treats you to a fanciful kitchen adventure as they invite you to create popular recipes from works of fiction. As they welcome you to their kitchen through an anthology of recipes from the stories they penned, you also are immersed in the world of their novels, as if you are part of the setting involved in the preparation of meals. What started as an imaginative thought has become an engaging culinary experience. Over 100 tried and tested recipes are included in this cookbook with passage references from the books where you can find each recipe. If you are not yet a fan of the trio's work of fiction, these recipes will get you started.

The Fiction Kitchen Trio Cookbook is sure to add more zest to your reading habits. The experience teaches that food and literature have a divine combination. Sarah M. Eden, Traci Hunter Abramson, and Sian Ann Bessey give you a fun experience—re-creating recipes from their stories as a way to make reading more immersive, educational, and delicious. I recreated Saint Squad Sliders when some friends came over to my place, and they couldn't help praising the sandwiches while their mouths were full. Being able to follow a recipe is a skill worth acquiring. It's an indulging exercise, a great way to bring family and friends together and enjoy these recipes. Eden, Abramson, and Bessey help to equip you with such skills using their easy-to-follow recipes, plus it gives you an increased interest in their books. Read it and try creating the recipes. The book is as interesting as it is delicious."

—*Readers' Favorite* five-star review

Table of Contents

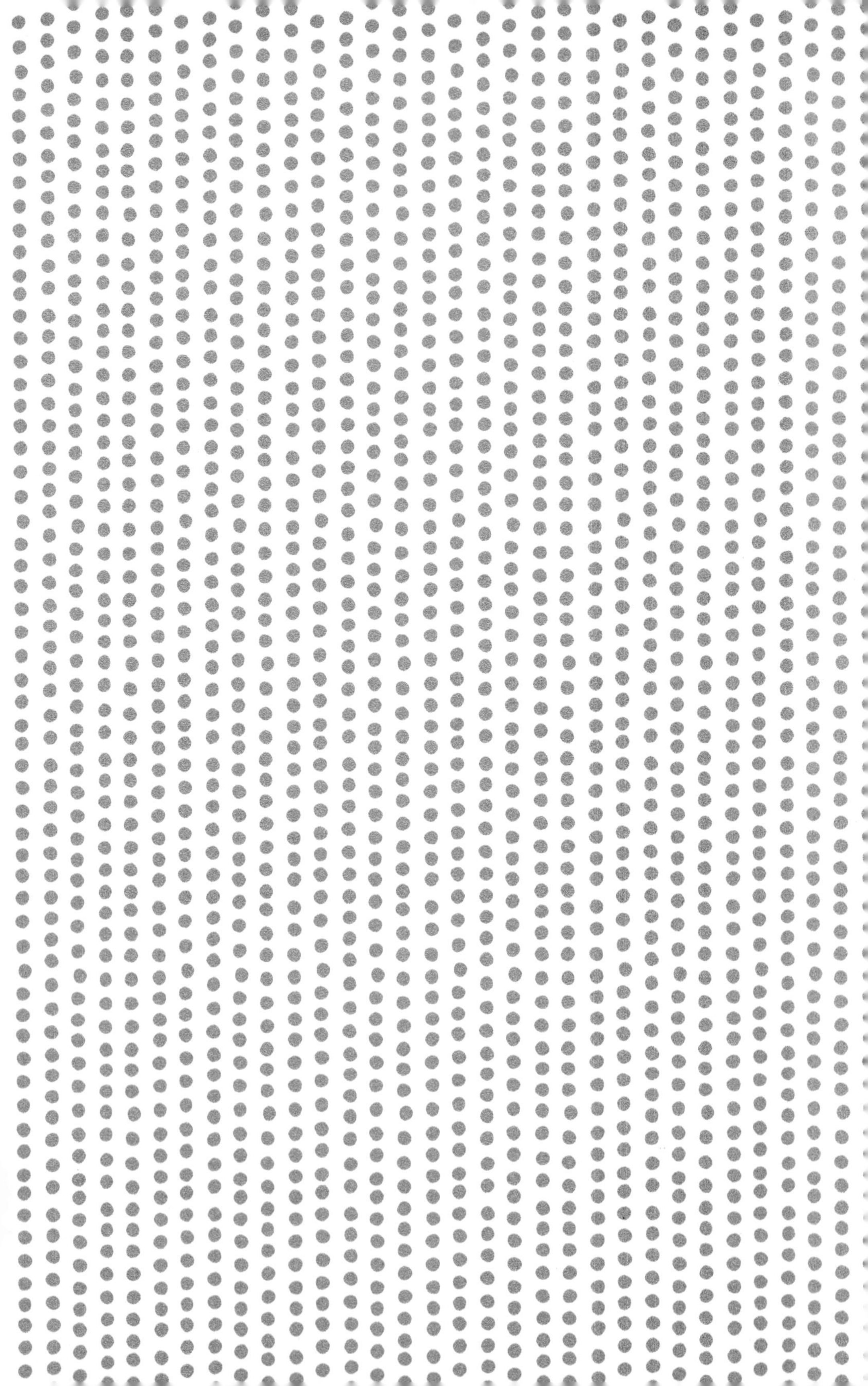

APPETIZERS AND BEVERAGES

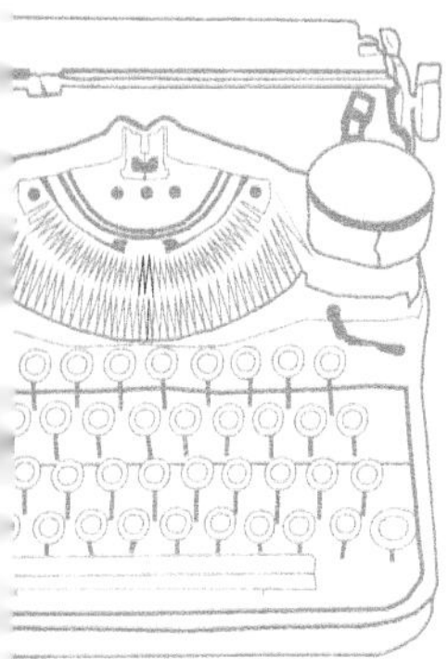

"Riley said to share."

"I did share."

"Giving me two isn't sharing." Quinn waved his hand impatiently through the air. "That's barely an appetizer."

"These *are* appetizers."

"What is it?" Craig asked.

"Those little potato and cheese things Riley makes," Tristan said.

Damian's eyes lit up. "The ones her mom made for the Fourth of July?"

"Yeah," Tristan said.

"I like those."

Covert Ops
Traci Hunter Abramson

Potato Bites

24 small redskin potatoes, washed
¾ cup butter, softened
½ teaspoon seasoned salt
¼ teaspoon garlic salt
2½ ounces Boursin cheese
½ cup cooked bacon, crumbled

Preheat oven to 425°F.

While oven is preheating, poke each potato with a fork about four times. Place potatoes on a baking sheet and bake for 45 minutes. Test with a fork to make sure potatoes are tender. If needed, bake for a few more minutes until tender. Remove potatoes from oven and allow to cool for 5 minutes.

Lower oven temperature to 400°F.

Cut each potato in half. Scoop out the center, leaving the skin intact. Set skins aside, and reserve for later.

Mash potato insides and mix with butter, seasoned salt, garlic salt, Boursin cheese, and bacon crumbles. Scoop potato mixture back into potato skins and place on a baking sheet. Bake for 10 minutes or until heated through.

Yields 48 potato bites.

It's edit time. What can I make that's fast, easy, and tastes great? This recipe.

Sian Ann Bessey

Bean Salsa

1 (15-ounce) can black beans, drained
1 (15-ounce) can black-eyed peas, drained
1 bunch cilantro, rinsed and chopped
4–5 medium tomatoes, chopped
6 ounces frozen white corn
8 ounces Italian dressing
1 avocado, diced

An hour before eating, mix beans, peas, cilantro, tomatoes, corn, and dressing together in a medium-sized bowl, cover, and place in refrigerator. Immediately before serving, add diced avocado and gently mix again. Serve with tortilla chips or quesadillas.

Yields 12–16 servings.

The waiter arrived and set a plate of stuffed mushrooms in between them.

Cassie picked up her fork and lifted one onto her plate. She cut it in half and took a bite. "Mmm." She chewed, savoring. After she swallowed, she speared the other half. "Okay, this is seriously amazing."

"I know. Patrice has been trying to get this recipe for over a year."

"I can see why." Cassie lowered her voice. "Maybe she should get Garrett to issue a royal command."

Royal Heir
Traci Hunter Abramson

Crab-Stuffed Mushrooms

¾ pound white or baby portabella mushrooms
3 ounces cream cheese, softened
½ cup crab meat
½ cup swiss cheese, finely shredded
¼ teaspoon Old Bay seasoning
Paprika to taste

Preheat oven to 350°F.

Wash mushrooms and remove stems.

Dice stems and mix with cream cheese, crab meat, swiss cheese, and Old Bay seasoning.

Stuff mushroom caps with crab meat mixture and place filled caps on baking sheet. Sprinkle with paprika.

Bake for 15–20 minutes.

Yields 14–18 stuffed mushrooms.

Brogan stopped at a roasted nut cart and purchased two bags of hot chestnuts.

Vera bumped him with her shoulder. "You spoil me with these, you know."

"You deserve a spot of spoiling. Besides that, the Newports aren't wealthy people, no matter that they've an impressive address. I can't say we'll be offered anything to eat while we're there, and I've no wish for you to be hungry."

She accepted the offering with a grateful smile. "Very thoughtful of you."

He dipped his head in an overdone impersonation of a fine society gentleman. "I am terribly gallant."

"Or just terribly hungry."

The Merchant and the Rogue
Sarah M. Eden

A few enterprising merchants had chosen to benefit from the large gathering by selling warm buns, nuts roasted in honey, apples, and pears.

To Win a Lady's Heart
Sian Ann Bessey

Honey-Roasted Nuts

1 tablespoon butter
1 tablespoon honey
8 ounces raw, unsalted nuts (a variety works well)
½ teaspoon paprika
½ teaspoon salt

Preheat oven to 300°F.

Cover a baking sheet with parchment paper.

Place butter and honey in a microwave-safe glass dish and heat until butter is melted, approximately 10–15 seconds. Add the nuts and paprika. Toss to coat.

Spread mixture evenly on a prepared baking sheet. Roast in oven for about 30 minutes, stirring every 10 minutes.

Remove nuts from oven and pour onto a piece of waxed paper. Sprinkle with salt and allow to cool. Store in an airtight container.

Yields 6–8 servings.

"Do they have those ham slider things that they serve in the restaurant here?" Tristan asked.

"They do," Skyler said.

Tristan pointed at the printed menu. "Put those on the list."

Craig laughed. "I'll see what I can do."

Covert Ops
Traci Hunter Abramson

Saint Squad Sliders

Sandwiches:
12 hawaiian dinner rolls
¼ cup mayonnaise
¼ cup Miracle Whip
12 pieces ham
12 small slices swiss cheese

Sauce:
¼ cup butter, melted
2 teaspoons yellow mustard
2 teaspoons minced onion
¼ teaspoon Worcestershire sauce

Preheat oven to 350°F.

For the sandwiches:
Cut rolls in half.

In a small bowl, combine mayonnaise and Miracle Whip. Spread mixture inside the top and bottom of each roll. Add a piece of ham and a slice of cheese inside each roll to make a miniature sandwich.

Place sandwiches in a 9 x 9-inch baking pan, arranging each sandwich close to the others.

For the sauce:
In a medium bowl, combine melted butter, mustard, onion, and Worcestershire sauce. Pour mixture evenly over sandwiches until the tops are covered. It's not necessary to use all the sauce.

Cover pan with foil. Bake in oven for 12–15 minutes or until heated through and cheese is melted. Uncover and bake for an additional 3 minutes. Serve warm.

Yields 12 sliders.

Mr. Hadford took a sip, swooshed the cider around in his mouth for a few seconds, and then swallowed. He eyed Adam silently and then took another drink. Adam forced himself to remain still. Mr. Hadford set his mug on the nearest barrel. "I wish to raise the order for my personal cellar from one barrel to three." He pointed at his empty cup. "That is by far the best cider I have ever tasted."

An Alleged Rogue
Sian Ann Bessey

Apple Cider

6 Fuji or Gala apples, cored and cubed
1 Granny Smith apple, cored and cubed
2 cinnamon sticks
5 cups water
Pinch of salt
2–4 teaspoons brown sugar*

Place apples, cinnamon sticks, water, and salt in a slow cooker. Cook on low for at least 8 hours or overnight.

Using a slotted spoon, remove the solids and press through a fine sieve to extract as much juice as possible.

Pour extracted juice and the liquid remaining in the slow cooker into a jug. Stir in brown sugar until dissolved. If necessary, add a little water to dilute the cider. Serve warm.

*Apples vary in sweetness. Taste the apple cider before adding brown sugar, and adjust the amount accordingly.

Yields 4 cups.

"Would you like me to fetch you a glass of raspberry shrub?" [Charlie] asked. "I understand the duchess's recipe is considered the very best in London."

Charming Artemis
Sarah M. Eden

Raspberry Shrub

More acidic, closer to the 18th-century version:
1 cup raspberries, fresh or frozen
1 cup white sugar
1 cup white or apple cider vinegar

More mild, modern version:
1 cup raspberries, fresh or frozen
1⅛ cups white sugar
½ cup rice wine vinegar

In a quart-size mason jar, combine raspberries and sugar. Place a square of parchment paper over the top and screw the lid on tight. Place the jar in the refrigerator for 3 days, stirring once each day.

On the third day, add vinegar. Stir well. Replace parchment paper and lid and put jar back in the refrigerator for an additional 2–3 days, stirring once each day.

On the final day, stir very well. Strain any remaining berries from the syrupy mixture. Place syrup in an airtight container in the refrigerator. Will stay good for up to a month.

To serve: Add syrup* to seltzer water, flavored carbonated water, lemon-lime soda, etc., to create a tart drink. Serve cold.

*Every hostess had her own variation on shrub, and some were quite proud of theirs. Try different ratios until you find a sharpness or sweetness that you like best.
My preferred ratio:
¼ cup ice
¾ cup seltzer water (plain or lemon-lime flavored)
3 tablespoons mild syrup or 2 tablespoons acidic syrup

Yields approximately ¾ cup syrup.

Kade let out a sigh. "I really hate it when national security gets in the way of dessert."

"It's a challenge." Renee led the way inside. "Tell you what. I'll make you one of those peanut butter smoothies you like."

Mistaken Reality
Traci Hunter Abramson

Peanut Butter Smoothie

¾ cup milk or almond milk
1½ cups ice
3 tablespoons peanut butter
1 tablespoon cocoa powder (optional)
1 scoop vanilla or peanut butter protein powder
1 banana

Combine ingredients in blender. Blend until mixed thoroughly.

Yields approximately 24 ounces.

"I was going to make a smoothie. Do you want one?"

"It depends on what kind you're making. I'm not eating anything green. Spinach belongs in salads, not in drinks."

"I was thinking strawberry and banana."

"I can do that."

Mistaken Reality
Traci Hunter Abramson

Strawberry-Banana Smoothie

2 cups strawberries
1 banana
2 tablespoons sugar
1½ cups ice
½ cup water or milk (optional)*

Combine ingredients in blender. Blend until mixed thoroughly.

*Note: If using frozen strawberries, add ½ cup water or milk so the ingredients will blend more smoothly.

Yields approximately 24 ounces.

"McDonalds?" Bianca suggested hopefully.

Jay shook his head. "Nice try. Besides, we already had dinner."

"We had a smoothie. With spinach in it," Bianca said pointedly. "I can't believe you convinced me to try that."

"It's healthy, and it'll give you lots of energy."

"It was green."

Code Word
Traci Hunter Abramson

And yes, this is the fuel I use to get through the day.

Traci Hunter Abramson

Traci's Survival Smoothie

1 cup almond milk
2 cups ice
1 tablespoon flaxseed
3 tablespoons unsweetened applesauce
2 tablespoons blueberries
3 tablespoons unsweetened peanut butter
1 medium carrot, peeled and sliced, or approximately 8 baby carrots
½ cup spinach
1 banana

Combine ingredients in blender. Blend until mixed thoroughly.

Yields approximately 32 ounces.

"You'd best get something to eat right away, then," Giles said, raising his cup. "The drinking chocolate is marvelous."

A Season of Hope
Sian Ann Bessey

Woodcroft Hall's Drinking Chocolate

⅔ cup sugar
⅔ cup powdered sugar
⅔ cup cocoa powder
½ cup powdered milk

To make mix:
Combine ingredients in a plastic bag and shake until well combined.

To make drinking chocolate:
Add 2–3 tablespoons of mix to 1 cup of hot water. For a richer drink, add mix to 1 cup of hot milk or ½ cup hot water and ½ cup hot milk.

Yields 2½ cups drinking chocolate mix, or 15–20 servings.

Tip: The advantage to making your own mix is that you can adjust the sweetness to your taste. Feel free to tweak the amount of sugar in this recipe until you think it's just right.

BREAKFASTS & BREADS

He retrieved their food and set it on their table.

"What did you get?"

"A ham-and-cheese crepe and a mushroom quiche."

"Those both look good."

"I thought if I offered to share, you'd let me try a bite of your soup."

"I think I can be persuaded," Brooke said. "But I was serious about saving room for dessert."

A Change of Fortune
Traci Hunter Abramson

Mushroom Quiche

3 tablespoons butter
½ cup onion, chopped
½ pound mushrooms, sliced
1 pound cheddar cheese, shredded
1 pound monterey jack cheese, shredded
12 eggs
16 ounces sour cream
1½ teaspoons seasoned salt

Preheat oven to 375°F.

Melt butter in a medium saucepan over medium heat. Add onion and sauté for 3 minutes. Add mushrooms and sauté until all vegetables are soft.

In a 9 x 13-inch baking dish, layer ⅓ of the cheddar cheese, followed by ⅓ of the monterey jack cheese. Spoon half of the mushroom-onion mixture on top and spread evenly.

Repeat with another layer of both cheeses, followed by the remaining mushroom-onion mixture. Top with the last ⅓ of both cheeses.

In a large bowl, beat eggs with a wire whisk. Add sour cream and seasoned salt. Mix until well blended. Pour over cheese mixture.

Bake for 40–50 minutes or until top is beginning to brown and the center is set and no longer jiggles.

Note: This quiche does not have a crust, but if desired, repeat the above process using two pie pans and pre-baked pastry shells. Bake for 35–45 minutes.

Yields 12 servings.

"I don't think I could eat another bite," Janessa said, laying a hand on her stomach. She lowered her voice and peeked through the door to make sure the caterers were indeed gone. "By the way, I much prefer your Quiche Florentine."

Patrice laughed. "So do I."

Royal Target
Traci Hunter Abramson

Patrice's Quiche Florentine

2 tablespoons butter
½ cup onion, chopped
2 cups fresh spinach, chopped
8 ounces swiss cheese, shredded
1 (9-inch) pre-baked pastry shell
4 eggs
⅓ cup mayonnaise
3 ounces cream cheese, softened
½ teaspoon dried minced onion
½ teaspoon seasoned salt
¼ teaspoon salt

Preheat oven to 350°F.

Melt butter in a medium saucepan. Add chopped onion and sauté for 3–5 minutes or until translucent. Add spinach and sauté until spinach just turns dark green.

Layer ⅓ of the cheese followed by ⅓ of the spinach-onion mixture in pastry shell. Repeat two more times.

In a large bowl, beat eggs with a wire whisk. Stir in mayonnaise, cream cheese, dried minced onion, seasoned salt, and salt. Mix well. Pour into pastry shell over cheese-and-spinach mixture.

Bake for 40–45 minutes or until set. The quiche should be a light golden brown, and it should no longer jiggle in the center.

Yields 8 servings.

"I got the stuff for eggs Benedict for breakfast tomorrow." Tara turned with a grin. "I figured you owed me after I picked this up for you."

"What is it?" Curiosity had CJ moving toward the kitchen.

"A laptop. I thought you might want to get online and check out when the next swim meet is."

The Deep End
Traci Hunter Abramson

Eggs Benedict

Hollandaise sauce:
2 egg yolks
1 tablespoon lemon juice
½ cup cold butter, divided

4 pre-cut ham steaks (approximately the size of an english muffin)
2 tablespoons butter or margarine
2 english muffins (4 halves)
4 eggs

For the Hollandaise sauce:
Combine yolks and lemon juice in a pan. Add ¼ cup butter; stir constantly over low heat until butter is melted. Stir in remaining butter until sauce thickens. Set aside. Cover to keep warm.

For the eggs benedict:
Turn oven to broil setting.

Using 1 tablespoon of butter, lightly butter the english muffins and set aside.

In a large skillet, melt the remaining tablespoon of butter. Add eggs, being careful not to break the yolks. Add 1-2 tablespoons water. Cover skillet and cook eggs until a white film covers the yolks.

Meanwhile, microwave ham for about 1 minute.

Place English muffins under the broiler until toasted.

To assemble:
Place a slice of ham on each English muffin half. Top with an egg and Hollandaise sauce.

Yields 4 servings.

She was right. Eggs were better from the microwave. Or maybe it was all the cheese she added. He scooped more eggs onto his plate, took another bite, and tried to remember why Jocelyn needed to leave.

In Harm's Way
Traci Hunter Abramson

Jocelyn's Scrambled Eggs

6 eggs
¼ cup milk
1 teaspoon seasoned salt
1 tablespoon butter or margarine
1 ounce cream cheese
1 cup colby or monterey jack cheese, shredded

In a microwave-safe bowl, whisk together eggs, milk, and seasoned salt. Cut the butter and cream cheese into small chunks and drop individual pieces into the egg batter. Gently stir in shredded cheese.

Cook in microwave for 45 seconds, then stir eggs with a fork. Repeat two more times.

Continue cooking in the microwave, now stirring after every 25 seconds for four cycles. When eggs are nearly done, reduce cooking time to 15-second intervals. Remove from microwave as soon as eggs are no longer runny. Do not overcook. Eggs will continue cooking in the bowl.

Serve immediately.

Yields 4 servings.

"Mother is in the kitchen. The moment she knows you are here, she will stop what she is doing to join you in the parlor." Her eyes twinkled. "On the other hand, we could dispense with all polite protocols and relocate to the kitchen, which would be much closer to the hot griddlecakes."

Philip grinned. After five years in the West Indies, he had become altogether too comfortable with ignoring social conventions. Besides, no one made griddlecakes as well as Mrs. Nesbitt. "When it comes to your mother's griddlecakes, I can guarantee I have not changed a bit," he said. "Lead me to the kitchen."

A Season of Hope
Sian Ann Bessey

Mrs. Nesbitt's Griddlecakes

1 cup all-purpose flour
½ cup whole wheat flour
2½ teaspoons baking powder
2 tablespoons sugar
¾ teaspoon salt
1 egg, slightly beaten
3 tablespoons butter, melted
1 cup milk

Combine dry ingredients. Add slightly beaten egg, melted butter, and milk. Stir until smooth. Batter should be barely thin enough to pour. Add more milk if necessary.

Pour into 4–5-inch circles on a warm, greased griddle or frying pan on medium heat. When bubbles form, flip cake to brown the other side. Serve warm with butter and syrup or with fruit and whipped cream.

Yields 8–10 griddlecakes.

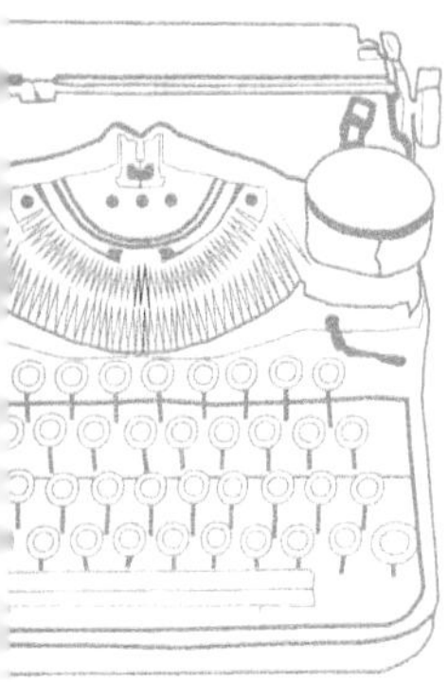

I grew up eating these muffins, and after adjusting the recipe for family allergies, I have made these for my own children. With a little prep time, this recipe provides weeks of hot breakfasts with minimal morning effort. It is a lifesaver on hectic mornings.

Sarah M. Eden

Dairy-free, Egg-free, Nut-free

6-week Breakfast Muffins

1 tablespoon vinegar
Approximately 1 cup non-dairy milk
1 (15-ounce) box Raisin Bran cereal
3 cups sugar
5 cups flour
5 teaspoons baking soda
2 teaspoons salt
1 cup canola oil
1 cup applesauce
1 teaspoon baking powder

Pour vinegar into a 1-cup measuring cup. Fill measuring cup the rest of the way with non-dairy milk. Let sit for 10 minutes or until the milk begins to curdle. (If dairy allergies are not an issue in your house, substitute the vinegar and non-dairy milk with 1 cup of buttermilk.)

In a very large bowl, mix Raisin Bran cereal, sugar, flour, baking soda, and salt. Add oil, applesauce, baking powder, and non-dairy milk mixture (or buttermilk). Stir until well combined.

Store in a covered container and use as needed. Can be stored in the refrigerator for up to 6 weeks.

When ready to make muffins:
Preheat oven to 400°F. Fill paper-lined muffin tins ⅔ full with muffin mixture. Bake for 18–20 minutes.

Yields approximately 5 dozen.

Selecting a muffin from her bread box for breakfast, she headed outside, her gaze drawn to Ace's boat moored beside hers. She broke off a bite of muffin and savored the contrast of tart blueberries and the sweetness of crumb topping.

Sanctuary
Traci Hunter Abramson

Blueberry Muffins

Streusel:
¼ cup sugar
2 tablespoons flour
1 tablespoon cold butter or margarine
1 ounce cream cheese

Muffins:
3 ounces cream cheese, softened
⅓ cup sour cream
¾ cup sugar
¼ cup vegetable oil
½ teaspoon vanilla

1 egg, beaten
1½ cups flour
1½ teaspoons baking powder
¼ teaspoon salt
½ cup frozen blueberries

Preheat oven to 350°F.

For the streusel:
In a small bowl, combine ¼ cup sugar and 2 tablespoons flour. With a fork, cut in butter or margarine and 1 ounce cream cheese until mixture resembles coarse crumbs. Set aside.

For the muffins:
In a large bowl, combine softened cream cheese, sour cream, and ¾ cup sugar. Stir in vegetable oil, vanilla, and egg. Add remaining ingredients and mix until combined into a moist batter.

Spoon batter evenly into 12 muffin cups. Top each muffin cup with streusel. Bake for 20–22 minutes.

Yields 12 muffins.

A spray of daisies smiled from the middle of the basket, and an assortment of individually wrapped muffins encircled the flowers.

"Blast him," Kylie muttered.

Jill just raised an eyebrow when she drew out the card and extended it to Kylie. "It's for you."

Kylie snatched the card and tossed it onto the table unopened. "Thanks."

"Who was at the door?" Brooke asked, walking into the kitchen. "Oh, wow."

"At least read the card," Jill suggested.

"I don't want to read the card." Kylie stood up from the table, annoyance edging her voice. "I'm going to swim."

Ripple Effect
Traci Hunter Abramson

Streusel Muffins

Flaxseed mixture* (egg substitute):
1 tablespoon ground flaxseed
3 tablespoons cold water

Streusel:
2 tablespoons sugar
1 tablespoon flour
¼ teaspoon cinnamon
2 tablespoons butter or margarine

Muffins:
1¾ cups flour
½ cup sugar
2 teaspoons baking powder
¼ teaspoon salt
⅔ cup applesauce
⅓ cup vegetable oil
1 teaspoon vanilla

Preheat oven to 375°F.

For flaxseed mixture (egg substitute):
In a small bowl, mix ground flaxseed and cold water. Place in refrigerator for 15 minutes.

For the streusel:
In a small bowl, mix 2 tablespoons sugar, 1 tablespoon flour, and cinnamon. Cut butter into 4 or 5 pieces. Then, using a fork, cut butter or margarine into the other ingredients until the mixture resembles coarse crumbs. Set aside.

For the muffins:
In a medium-sized bowl, combine 1¾ cups flour, ½ cup sugar, baking powder, and salt. Add flaxseed mixture (or egg), applesauce, vegetable oil, and vanilla. Stir until combined into a moist batter.

Spoon batter evenly into 12 muffin cups. Sprinkle each muffin cup with streusel. Bake for 14–18 minutes or until a toothpick inserted in the center comes out clean.

*Note: One beaten egg can be substituted for the flaxseed mixture.

Yields 12 muffins.

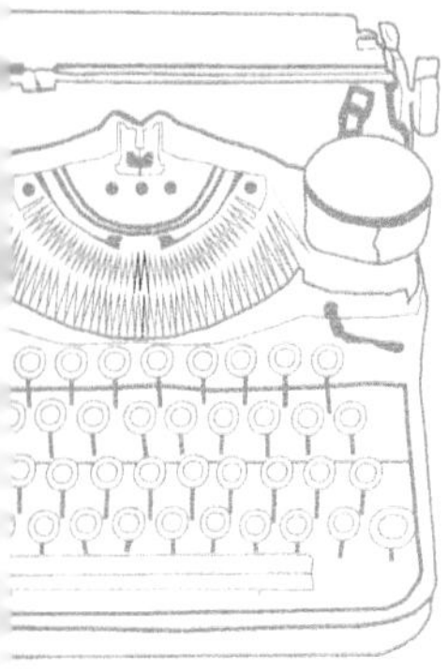

"Good day, Your Grace. I wondered how long it would take before you made your way into the kitchen. I believe you can smell Chelsea buns cooking all the way in that workshop of yours."

Somewhat surprised by his cook's familiar greeting, Rosalind glanced at Sebastian to see him grinning.

"I confess, when I became too old to sneak down here without suffering a reprimand from my governess, I put Vickers under oath to inform me whenever Chelsea buns were coming out of the oven," he said.

An Unfamiliar Duke
Sian Ann Bessey

The Duke of Kelbrook's Chelsea Buns

Bread dough:
⅓ cup powdered milk
½ cup sugar
½ cup butter, melted
1 cup hot water
1½ tablespoons yeast
½ cup warm water
3 large eggs, beaten
½ tablespoon salt
5–6 cups flour

Filling:
2 tablespoons butter, softened
½ cup brown sugar
4 teaspoons cinnamon, or to taste
1 cup golden raisins
½ cup raisins

Glaze:
¼ cup sugar
3 tablespoons water

For the bread dough:
In a large bowl, combine powdered milk, sugar, melted butter, and hot water.

In a small bowl, stir yeast into ½ cup warm water. Once yeast has formed a foamy layer, mix into beaten eggs, then add to milk mixture. Add the salt and enough flour into the milk mixture to make a soft dough. Knead for 5 minutes.

Place dough in a greased bowl, rotate dough so that it is greased on all sides, and cover with a cloth. Allow to rise until dough has doubled in bulk (45–60 minutes).

Cover two baking sheets with parchment paper. Punch down dough and divide into two. Roll each portion into a rectangle (approximately 16 x 10 inches).

For the filling:
On one rectangle of dough, spread half the softened butter and half the brown sugar. Sprinkle with 2 teaspoons cinnamon (or to taste), half the golden raisins, and half the raisins.

Starting with the long side, roll dough into a log and slice into approximately 1-inch pieces. Place slices face down on baking sheets, approximately 1 inch apart. Repeat the process with the second piece of dough.

Preheat oven to 350°F. Allow rolls to rise for about 30 minutes. Bake for 15–20 minutes or until golden brown.

For the glaze:
Mix the sugar and water together in a saucepan or microwave-safe bowl. Heat to boiling. Brush hot sugar water over the top of the rolls while still on the pan. Remove rolls to a wire racks to cool completely.

Yields 20–24 buns.

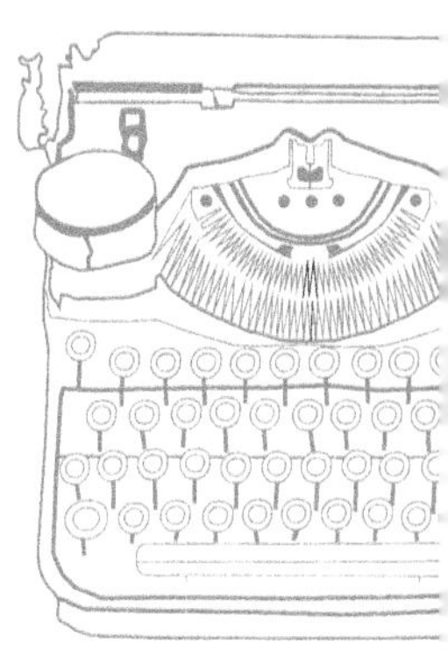

"Quinn, when people say the way to a man's heart is through his stomach, they must be talking about you."

"Your mom's cinnamon rolls are the best."

"I know. I grew up with them," Amy said.

Redemption
Traci Hunter Abramson

Katherine's Cinnamon Rolls

Bread dough:
½ teaspoon sugar
¼ cup warm water
1 tablespoon yeast
¼ cup sugar
½ teaspoon salt
1 cup warm milk
3 tablespoons butter, softened
1 large egg, beaten
Pinch of baking soda (1/16 teaspoon)
3½–4 cups flour

Filling:
3 tablespoons butter, melted
⅔ cup sugar
2 teaspoons cinnamon

Cream cheese icing:
4 ounces cream cheese, softened
¼ cup butter, softened
1 teaspoon vanilla
1¼ cups powdered sugar
1 tablespoon milk (optional)

For the bread dough:
Combine ½ teaspoon sugar with ½ cup warm water. Sprinkle yeast on top. Let sit for 5 minutes.

In a larger bowl, combine ¼ cup sugar, salt, warm milk, 3 tablespoons softened butter, and egg. Add yeast mixture to milk and egg mixture. Add flour 1 cup at a time until the dough is only slightly sticky. Cover bowl with a cloth and allow dough to rise for 45 minutes to an hour or until doubled in size. Punch down dough. If it is too sticky to handle easily, add another ¼–½ cup flour and knead into dough.

Grease a 9 x 13-inch pan. Place dough on a lightly floured surface. Roll into a 12 x 18-inch rectangle.

Preheat oven to 350°F.

For the filling:
Using a basting brush, spread the melted butter on the top of the rolled-out dough. Mix ⅔ cup sugar with cinnamon and sprinkle evenly on top of the buttered dough.

Starting at the 12-inch end, roll the dough. Pinch the edge of dough to seal it closed. Cut the rolled dough into twelve 1-inch portions. Place each roll, face down, into the pan. Repeat the process with the other half of the dough.

Bake for 18–22 minutes or until a light golden brown.

For the icing:
Combine cream cheese, ¼ cup butter, and vanilla. Cream together until well blended. Add powdered sugar, ¼ to ½ cup at a time, until mixture reaches a creamy consistency. If desired, add 1 tablespoon milk.

Allow rolls to cool for 10 minutes before icing.

Yields 12 cinnamon rolls.

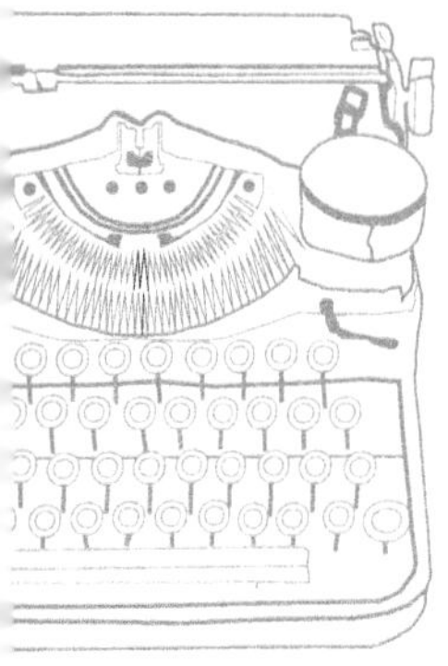

Mariposa nearly jumped out of her skin when something was, without warning, laid on her lap. Her eyes darted in the direction of the delivery. She could not say what she'd expected to see, but the sight of two scones lying inauspiciously on a napkin caught her entirely by surprise. Who had put them there, and why?

She raised her eyes enough to look at the passenger next to her on the seat. Instantly, her heart leapt into her throat. Jason. He hadn't left her.

A Fine Gentleman
Sarah M. Eden

Levi gave Janessa a hug. "Don't get too royal on me."

"I'll do my best." She flashed a smile. "But just so you know, I may have used my royalness to score you those scones you like so much."

"Patrice made blueberry scones?"

"She did."

"That does it. I think you rank as my best friend again."

Royal Heir
Traci Hunter Abramson

Scones

2¾ cups all-purpose flour
⅓ cup granulated sugar
¾ teaspoon salt
1½ tablespoons baking powder
½ cup butter, cold, cubed
1½ cups small, dried fruit, such as raisins, currants, sultanas, dried blueberries, etc. (optional)
2 large eggs
2 teaspoons vanilla extract
½ cup milk + extra for brushing on scones
Ultra-fine sugar for sprinkling on scones

In a large mixing bowl, whisk together the flour, sugar, salt, and baking powder. Use a handheld dough blender (or your fingers) to mix in butter until the mixture is crumbly. (If using, stir in the dried fruit.)

In a smaller bowl, whisk the eggs, vanilla extract, and ½ cup milk together. Add to the dry ingredients. Mix well, scraping the sides, until a moist but firm dough is created.

On a lightly floured surface, roll out dough to ¾-inch thick. Use a round biscuit or pastry cutter to cut out 8 scones. Place on a parchment-paper-lined baking sheet and place in the refrigerator for 30 minutes.

Preheat the oven to 400°F. Pull scones out of refrigerator and brush tops with milk, then sprinkle with ultra-fine sugar. Return to the refrigerator until oven is fully heated.

Bake for 18–20 minutes until tops are golden brown. Remove from oven and move scones from pan to a wire cooling rack. Serve warm. These scones are especially good served with clotted cream and jam.

Yields 8 scones.

I went through a lot of trial and error before figuring out how to make a good, authentic clotted cream, but it was well worth it. We eat it mostly on scones but have also been known to put it on waffles, pancakes, and American-style biscuits. It isn't labor intensive; it simply takes time. Enjoy!

Sarah M. Eden

Clotted Cream

Heavy whipping cream (It is crucial that the cream not be "ultra-pasteurized.")

Preheat oven to lowest temperature (generally 170°–180°F).

Pour enough heavy cream into a glass casserole dish to achieve 2 inches of height. Place pan, uncovered, in the oven for 10–12 hours. Check the cream at the 8-hour mark, and every hour thereafter. Cream is done when it has only just begun to turn golden.

Remove from the oven and allow to cool until room temperature. Place in the refrigerator for an additional 8 hours.

Skim the thick cream off the top of the dish—a translucent white liquid will be beneath the thickened cream—and place in a jar or bowl. Stir well until the cream reaches the consistency of a whipped butter. If cream is too thick, add small amounts of remaining liquid until desired consistency is achieved.

Store in an airtight container in the refrigerator for up to a week.

Yield:
An 8 x 8 pan will use approximately 2–3 cups of heavy cream and will yield approximately 1–1½ cups of clotted cream.

A 9 x 13 pan will use approximately 5–6 cups of heavy cream and will yield approximately 2–2½ cups of clotted cream.

"What is it about your mam's bara brith that has people dreaming about it?" she said.

Lewis grinned. "I don't know. She wins ribbons at the county show whenever she enters, and I have yet to taste any better."

One Last Spring
Sian Ann Bessey

Mair's Bara Brith

2 cups dried fruit (raisins, sultanas, golden raisins, craisins, etc.)
6 tablespoons butter
1 cup brown sugar
1¼ ounces water
1 teaspoon mixed spice*
2½ cups flour
4 teaspoons baking powder
1¼ teaspoons salt
1 egg

*This is a British seasoning, not to be mistaken for allspice. If mixed spice is unavailable, a similar blend can be made by mixing together the following:

1 tablespoon cinnamon
1 teaspoon coriander
1 teaspoon nutmeg
½ teaspoon ginger
¼ teaspoon allspice
¼ teaspoon cloves

In a saucepan, heat dried fruit, butter, brown sugar, water, and mixed spice. Simmer for 10 minutes. Pour into a bowl with a lid. Cover and allow to cool overnight.

Preheat oven to 300°F

In a separate bowl, combine flour, baking powder, and salt. Add egg and fruit mixture and mix until well blended.

Pour into a greased 8 x 4-inch bread pan. Bake for 1½ hours. Allow to cool for 5–10 minutes and then remove from pan to cool completely on a wire rack.

Serve sliced and spread with butter.

Yields 1 loaf.

"They are one of our cook's specialties," Jane said. "I've not known anyone who has tried her spiced buns and not loved them."

An Uncommon Earl
Sian Ann Bessey

"That was my home for ten days. Ten miserable, terrible days. I kept hidden and quiet, sneaking out only to try to find food. Jim came upon me in the alley behind the bakery when I was searching through crates for any bits of flour or dough that might have been there. He didn't say anything for a long moment but simply looked at me as though he were reading all the details of my life." She wrapped her fingers more firmly around Miles's, her eyes focused off in the distance. "He bought a half-penny bun from the baker and gave it to me. He said I didn't need to say anything or tell him anything; he simply could feel that I needed help. There was something about him that I still can't even explain. But I knew in that moment that I didn't have to be afraid of him. We sat on a bench, and he told me he could see that I was in trouble and would help in any way he could."

For Elise
Sarah M. Eden

Spiced Buns

2¼ cups whole milk
7 cups flour
½ cup plus 2 tablespoons sugar
2 teaspoons cinnamon
2 teaspoons mixed spice*
½ teaspoon cardamom
2 teaspoons salt
2 tablespoons yeast
2 large eggs
7 tablespoons butter, softened
1½ cups golden raisins
½ cup craisins
Zest of 1 small orange
Zest of 1 lemon

*This is a British seasoning, not to be mistaken for all-spice. If mixed spice is unavailable, a similar blend can be made by mixing together the following:

1 tablespoon cinnamon
1 teaspoon coriander
1 teaspoon nutmeg
½ teaspoon ginger
¼ teaspoon allspice
¼ teaspoon cloves

Heat the milk to just warm, then remove from stove.

In the bowl of a stand mixer,** combine the flour, sugar, spices, salt, and yeast. Make a well in the center and pour in the milk and eggs. Mix with the dough hook attachment until blended. Add softened butter and mix for an additional 5 minutes, until the dough is smooth and elastic.

Add the dried fruit and zests. Knead for another 3 minutes. Turn out into a large, greased bowl (dough will be sticky). Rotate so that dough is greased on all sides, then cover the bowl with plastic wrap. Allow to rise until doubled in size (about an hour).

Punch down dough and divide into 24 equal pieces. Form into balls and place 2 inches apart on baking sheets lined with parchment paper. Cover with plastic wrap and allow to rise until double in size (about 35–45 minutes).

Preheat oven to 375°F.

If you wish to use this recipe to make hot-cross buns, apply a paste cross to the risen balls of dough before placing in oven. (See recipe for paste below).

Bake for 15–20 minutes or until golden brown.

For the hot cross buns:
¼ cup water
¼ cup flour

Blend flour and water until it forms a smooth paste. Pour paste into a small plastic bag and, with a pair of scissors, snip off one corner (about ⅛ inch across). Holding the plastic bag in both hands, squeeze the paste through the small hole, drawing it across the top of the buns in a cross pattern.

If desired, while buns are cooking, make up glaze. When the buns come out of the oven, brush them with the glaze. Remove from pan and place on a wire rack to cool.

Optional glaze:
2 tablespoons sugar
1 tablespoon corn syrup
3 tablespoons water

Heat sugar, syrup, and water in a pan until boiling. Stir for about 2 minutes. Set aside to cool.

Yields 24 buns.

Tip: Slice the buns in half, toast them, and spread with butter.

**If you do not own a stand mixer, this recipe can be made by hand in a large bowl.

She found leftover soda bread from the evening meal and sliced it thin and even. Mr. Archer had already set out a small bowl of eggs and strips of bacon. Katie cooked up both, then browned the bread in the bacon drippings. 'Twas only one half of a true Ulster fry but would make a fine breakfast.

Longing for Home
Sarah M. Eden

Katie's Irish Soda Bread

450 grams flour (about 3–3½ cups)
1 teaspoon salt
1 teaspoon baking soda
200–300 milliliters buttermilk (about 1–1 ¼cups)

Preheat oven to 350°F.

Combine all dry ingredients. Once the oven is preheated, stir in buttermilk until the dough begins to hold together. You may have to add a small amount of extra buttermilk if the dough isn't wet enough to stick together. Dough will be lumpy and sticky. Turn out onto a floured surface and knead just enough to get a ball of dough, usually no more than 15 seconds. Over-kneading will ruin the dough.

Shape into a slightly domed circle. With a sharp knife, cut across the center of the dough twice to create an X on the top. Cut deeply, but be sure that you don't quite cut all the way through. This is important for allowing the bread to rise properly.

Place dough on a lightly floured baking sheet in the pre-heated oven. Bake for 10 minutes. Without taking the loaf out of the oven, lower the oven temperature to 300°F and bake for an additional 35–45 minutes (this additional time will include the time while the temperature is adjusting). When bread is done, it will sound hollow when thumped on the bottom.

Yields 1 loaf.

"You could make us some of your banana bread to take with us."

"I already have two loaves in the freezer."

Amaliya opened the freezer with every intention of thawing one out.

"Don't even think about getting into it now. I froze it to make sure you couldn't eat it right away."

"I was only going to eat one piece."

Dreams of Gold
Traci Hunter Abramson

Irresistible Banana Bread

½ cup butter or margarine, softened
1¼ cups sugar
2 eggs
1 teaspoon baking soda
¼ cup sour cream
2 bananas, mashed
1½ cups all-purpose flour
1 teaspoon vanilla
½ cup chocolate chips (optional)

Preheat oven to 325°F.

In a large bowl, combine butter or margarine and sugar. Add eggs. In a small bowl, combine baking soda and sour cream together. Let stand one minute. Add to sugar mixture. Add other ingredients in order, one at a time, and mix until combined.

Grease a loaf pan. Bake for 1 hour or until knife a inserted near center comes out clean.

Alternatively, grease an 8-cavity mini-loaf pan or a 12-count muffin pan, and divide batter equally. Bake for 20–25 minutes or until the tops of the loaves spring back to the touch.

Yields 1 loaf, 8 mini loaves, or 12 muffins.

Phoebe pulled back the cloth covering on the basket to reveal cheese and a loaf of fresh bread cut into thick slices.

An Alleged Rogue
Sian Ann Bessey

Artisan Bread

3 cups warm water
3 tablespoons yeast
2 tablespoons sugar
6–7 cups unbleached bread flour, divided
1½ tablespoons salt
2 tablespoons olive oil
Cornmeal for dusting
1 cup cold water

Mix the warm water, yeast, and sugar in the bowl of a stand mixer. Proof for 5 minutes. Add 6 cups of flour, salt, and oil. Mix with dough hook attachment until combined. Add additional flour until the dough pulls away from the sides of the bowl. Dough should still be slightly sticky. Knead for 2–3 minutes. Transfer dough to a large, greased bowl. Rotate so that the dough is greased on all sides. Cover bowl with plastic wrap and allow to rise for 1 hour.

Place a baking stone (or pizza stone) into the oven on the middle rack and heat oven to 450°F. Meanwhile, punch dough down and divide into three loaves. Shape into ovals and place each on a piece of parchment paper dusted with cornmeal. Using a sharp knife, slice 3 or 4 shallow diagonal cuts onto the tops of the loaves. Allow to sit for about 20 minutes.

Using the parchment paper to lift the risen loaves, set the dough and the paper onto the baking stone in the oven. Pour 1 cup cold water into a shallow pan and place on the rack below the baking stone. Close the oven door immediately. The steam generated by the cold water in the oven will form the bread's crust. Cook for 22–25 minutes.

Yields 3 loaves.

"I filled my father's snappin tin every morning until the day he died," she said. "Bread with jam or butter and an apple or carrot."

"I think your dad and I would have had a lot in common," Evan said, smiling back at her. "I'll have a butty and an apple."

Within the Dark Hills
Sian Ann Bessey

"Word will spread fast that buying your bread will save money, money that could be used to buy other things our families need. I daresay you'll quickly be filling orders for soda bread and brown bread and daily loaves. There aren't enough of us to make you rich by any means. But I'd say we'll keep you busy . . ."

"I'll have myself a regular bakery before too long." Katie liked the sound of it. To be an independent woman of business would be something indeed.

Longing for Home
Sarah M. Eden

Quick and Easy Wheat Bread

5 cups warm water
½ cup brown sugar
5 cups whole wheat flour
⅔ cup vegetable or canola oil
2 tablespoons yeast
1 tablespoon salt
7–8 cups bread flour

Grease four loaf pans and preheat oven to 170°F.

In the bowl of a large stand mixer, blend warm water, brown sugar, and whole wheat flour. Add oil and yeast. Mix with dough hook. Add salt and enough bread flour that the dough pulls away from the sides of the bowl. Knead for 5 minutes. The dough will be soft.

Using floured hands, divide the dough into four equal portions and shape each into an oval. Place dough into the prepared loaf pans and immediately place them in the warm oven. Allow to rise in the oven for 20–25 minutes (until dough rises above the edge of the pans).

Without taking the loaves out of the oven, increase the temperature to 350°F and bake for 30–35 minutes. Remove bread from pans and allow to cool on racks.

Yields 4 loaves.

Philip would not have believed that a simple parlor breakfast of tea and buttered toast would be one of the best he could ever remember having, but it was.

A Season of Hope
Sian Ann Bessey

Mrs. Nesbitt's Oat Bread

4 cups whole wheat flour
1 cup quick-cooking oats
2 tablespoons yeast
1 tablespoon salt
2¼ cups warm water
¼ cup honey
¼ cup butter, melted
1 egg
2–3 cups bread flour

In a large mixing bowl or the bowl of a stand mixer, combine whole wheat flour, oats, yeast, and salt.

Add warm water, honey, and melted butter to dry ingredients; beat until blended. Beat in egg until smooth. Mix in enough flour to form a stiff dough.

Turn dough onto a floured surface and knead until smooth and elastic, about 6–8 minutes (or do this in a stand mixer with a dough hook). Place dough in a greased bowl, turning once to grease top. Cover and let rise in a warm place until doubled, about 1 hour.

Punch dough down. Turn onto a lightly floured surface, divide dough into three equal portions, and shape into oval loaves. Place loaves on greased baking sheets. With a sharp knife, make three shallow diagonal cuts across the top of each loaf. Cover and let rise until doubled, about 30 minutes.

Preheat oven to 350°F.

Bake for 30–40 minutes or until browned. Remove from baking sheets and place on wire racks to cool.

Yields 3 loaves.

Making dinner for everyone had given him a little break. Whipping up some chicken and cornbread was a lot more appealing than sitting in a tree, watching for an intruder who would hopefully never come.

Safe House
Traci Hunter Abramson

Cornbread

2 cups yellow cornmeal
2 cups all-purpose flour
⅔ cup sugar
3 tablespoons baking powder
1½ teaspoons salt
4 large eggs
2 cups milk
½ cup vegetable oil

Preheat oven to 425°F.

In a large bowl, combine cornmeal, flour, sugar, baking powder, and salt. Stir in eggs, milk, and oil until mixture is just moist. Pour into a greased 9 x 13-inch baking dish. Bake for 25 minutes or until light golden brown.

Yields 12–15 servings.

If I don't have time to make rolls, this is the recipe I turn to. It turns a simple meal of soup or chili into something special. Even those who don't have to eat gluten-free love it.

Sian Ann Bessey

Gluten-Free Cornbread

1 cup milk
1 egg
¼ cup vegetable or canola oil
¼ teaspoon vinegar
⅓ cup potato starch
½ cup cornstarch
1 teaspoon salt
¼ teaspoon baking soda
1 tablespoon baking powder
¾ cup cornmeal
¼ cup sugar
½ teaspoon xanthan gum

Preheat oven to 375°F.

In a medium bowl, combine milk, egg, oil, and vinegar. Mix well. Add all other ingredients and mix well, being sure to remove any lumps. Batter will be thin.

Pour batter into greased 8 x 8-inch baking pan. Bake 25–30 minutes, until top is lightly browned, and a toothpick inserted into the center comes out clean.

Yields 8–10 servings.

Clinging to this little hint of normalcy, Matt grinned and walked into the kitchen. He slipped his arms around CJ's waist, gave her a kiss, and reached past her for a roll that was cooling on the counter.

CJ shook her head, trying not to laugh as he released her and tossed the hot bread from one hand to the other. "You're going to burn yourself one of these days."

"Nah."

The Deep End
Traci Hunter Abramson

Simple Dinner Rolls

¼ cup warm water
½ teaspoon sugar
1 tablespoon yeast
1 cup hot water
⅓ cup shortening
⅓ cup sugar
1 teaspoon salt
3¼–3½ cups bread flour

In a small bowl, combine ¼ cup warm water, ½ teaspoon sugar, and yeast. Set aside.

In a large bowl, combine 1 cup hot water, shortening, ⅓ cup sugar, and salt. Stir until the sugar and salt dissolve and shortening begins to melt. Stir in yeast mixture. Add flour one cup at a time. Dough should be slightly sticky.

Cover dough and let rise for 45 minutes to an hour or until double in size. Punch dough down and divide into 12 balls. Place on a baking sheet and cover. Let rise for an additional 45 minutes.

Preheat oven to 350°F.

Bake for 15–20 minutes until lightly golden brown.

Yields 12 rolls.

Paisley stood at the table, gingerly moving hot rolls from a baking dish to a serving bowl . . .

"Smells good." Cade couldn't think of anything else to say.

"I certainly hope it tastes good as well."

The Sheriffs of Savage Wells
Sarah M. Eden

Clover Rolls

4½ cups all-purpose flour, divided
1 package active dry yeast (about 2¼ teaspoons)
1 cup milk
⅓ cup butter
⅓ cup sugar
¾ teaspoon salt
2 large eggs, beaten

In a large mixing bowl, combine 2 cups of flour and the yeast. In a saucepan, heat and stir milk, butter, sugar, and salt until warm and the butter ***almost*** melts. Add warmed milk mixture to the flour-and-yeast mixture. Add eggs. Beat with a mixer on medium speed for 30 seconds, scraping the bowl to mix everything. Increase mixer speed to high and beat for 3 minutes. Stir in as much remaining flour as you can.

On a lightly floured surface, knead in enough of any remaining flour to make the dough somewhat stiff, while still elastic and smooth (generally 5–10 minutes). Shape into a ball. Place in a lightly greased bowl; turn over in the bowl so dough is lightly greased as well. Cover and let rise in a warm place for approximately 1 hour, until dough is about double in size.

Punch dough down and turn onto a lightly floured surface. Divide in half. Cover.

Lightly grease muffin cups of two 12-count muffin tins (24 total cups). Further divide dough into 72 equal-sized pieces. Roll each piece into a ball, pinching sides under to create a smooth top. Place three balls in each muffin cup (smooth sides up), creating a clover-like shape. Cover and let rise in a warm place for approximately 30 minutes, until about double in size.

Preheat oven to 375°F.

Bake for 12–15 minutes or until golden. Remove rolls from muffin tins and place on a wire rack to cool.

Yields 24 rolls.

She smelled the Indian flatbread Maya often made in the mornings, and her mouth watered. The minute Kari entered the kitchen, Maya waved at the built-in warming tray. "I saved you some naan. It's in there."

"Thanks." Kari grabbed a paper towel in lieu of a plate and retrieved a piece. She glanced over at Lauren, who was sitting at the counter. "Did you get some?"

"Yeah. I was just telling Maya she should think about hiring a cook so she'd have more free time."

Kari laughed. "Maya wouldn't want someone else messing up her kitchen." She took a bite and rolled her eyes with pleasure. "This is so good."

Chance for Home
Traci Hunter Abramson

Maya's Indian Flatbread (Naan)

1 teaspoon sugar
⅔ cup warm water
1 tablespoon yeast
2 tablespoons olive oil

½ cup plain or vanilla yogurt
1 egg
3 cups flour
½ teaspoon salt
3 tablespoons butter, melted

In a small bowl, combine sugar with warm water. Sprinkle yeast on top of water. Let sit for 5–10 minutes.

In another bowl, combine olive oil, yogurt, and egg. Mix thoroughly. Add yeast mixture.

In a large bowl, combine flour and salt. Add the mixture of wet ingredients and stir until dough starts to form. Knead dough by hand until surface becomes smooth. If dough is too sticky, add additional flour a quarter cup at a time until dough is manageable.

Cover dough with a damp cloth and let rise for one hour or until approximately double in size.

Divide dough into 8–10 equal pieces and roll into balls. With a rolling pin, roll each ball of dough into a circle approximately ¼-inch thick.

Heat large cast-iron or nonstick skillet over medium-high heat. Place one piece of dough in the skillet. When it bubbles and puffs up, turn the bread over. The bread should have dark brown spots that are typical of naan bread. When both sides have cooked, remove from skillet and brush with melted butter. Repeat with each piece of dough. As each one is cooked, stack and wrap in a tea towel to keep warm until time to serve. Serve warm.

Yields 8–10 pieces.

SOUPS, SALADS, & SIDES

Sitting beside Kester in a small room of a humble inn on the outskirts of an obscure village, reveling in the warmth of a humble pork and pulse stew and enjoying the company of two of the loveliest people in all the world, Violet didn't have to pretend to be content. She was genuinely joyous.

Lily of the Valley
Sarah M. Eden

**Pulse* is a term for dried legumes, such as lentils, and a "pork and pulse stew" is simply another term for a pork or ham and lentil stew.

Ham & Lentil Stew

1 tablespoon extra-virgin olive oil
1 cup celery, chopped
1 cup onion, chopped
1 cup carrots, cut into bite-size slices
2 cloves garlic, minced
1½ cups cooked ham, diced
1 cup dry lentils
¼ teaspoon dried thyme
½ teaspoon dried basil
½ teaspoon dried oregano
4 cups chicken or vegetable broth

1 (8-ounce) can tomato sauce
1 cup water
1 small bay leaf
½ teaspoon lemon juice
¼ teaspoon black pepper
1¼ teaspoons salt

Electric pressure cooker (such as Instant Pot®) directions:
Using sauté setting, sauté celery and onion in oil for 1–2 minutes. Add carrots and sauté for 3–4 minutes. Add garlic, sauté for 2 minutes.

Add ham, lentils, thyme, basil, oregano, broth, tomato sauce, and water. Stir in bay leaf.

Close and lock the lid. Cook on high pressure for 8 minutes. Allow a natural release of pressure once cooking is complete.

Before serving, remove bay leaf. Stir in lemon juice, pepper, and salt.

Stovetop directions:
In a large saucepan or dutch oven, sauté celery and onion in oil for 1–2 minutes. Add carrots and sauté for 3–4 minutes. Add garlic, sauté for 2 minutes.

Add thyme, basil, oregano, broth, tomato sauce, water, and bay leaf. Bring to a boil. Cover, reduce heat to medium-low, and simmer for 7 minutes.

Add ham and lentils. Return to a boil. Replace lid. Reduce heat and simmer on medium-low for 30 minutes.

Before serving, remove bay leaf. Stir in lemon juice, pepper, and salt.

Yields 6–8 servings.

Kade tasted a spoonful of chowder and rolled his eyes heavenward. Fresh seafood wasn't typically something he indulged in; the storage and preparation alone were enough to deter him.

Taking another bite, he decided he and Renee might have to rethink their meal plans. "This is really good."

"Thanks." Kristi nodded toward the kitchen. "I made plenty. You're welcome to take some home with you to heat up later."

"That would be great," Kade said.

"I hope you realize what a huge compliment it is that he even said anything," Renee chimed in. "In case you haven't noticed, Kade isn't big on making conversation."

"I'll talk to people who feed me."

Sanctuary
Traci Hunter Abramson

Clam Chowder

3 tablespoons butter
¼ cup onion, chopped
2 medium potatoes, cubed
1 stalk celery, chopped
2 tablespoons flour
2 (6.5-ounce) cans minced clams, with juice (or the equivalent of fresh)
2 cups water
2 teaspoons instant chicken bouillon
1 teaspoon Old Bay seasoning
½ teaspoon salt
⅛ teaspoon pepper (optional)
1 cup heavy cream

Melt butter in a large saucepan. Add onion and sauté until soft. Add potatoes and celery. Sauté for 1–2 minutes. Sprinkle with flour and stir. Add clams with juice, water, chicken bouillon, Old Bay seasoning, salt, and pepper. Bring to a boil.

Reduce heat and simmer on low for 15 minutes.

Add cream, stirring constantly while heating through for approximately 3 minutes. Serve hot.

*For a non-dairy version, substitute non-dairy margarine for the butter and coconut milk for the cream.

Yields 4–6 servings.

A taste of Wales when I need some inspiration from home.

Sian Ann Bessey

"She doesn't seem one to buckle under the weight of life, though clearly she's endured her share of difficulties." Ma glanced back at Biddy, who ate her soup as she listened to Patrick's continued stories. "She told me she's not had family in a long time and was ever so grateful to be included in this one, even for a short while. She must be terribly lonely."

Knowing now that she didn't have family of her own, he couldn't begrudge her that longing. But was the chance to be something of a daughter and sister to someone, even for a short while, the greatest pull she felt in this house? Heavens, he hoped not.

My Dearest Love
Sarah M. Eden

Cheesy Potato and Leek Soup

2½ pounds potatoes, peeled and cubed
2 leeks, white and light green parts, washed and thinly sliced
6 cups chicken broth
1 teaspoon salt
¼ teaspoon pepper
1 cup milk
1 tablespoon lemon juice
3 cups sharp cheddar cheese, grated

Combine potatoes, leeks, broth, salt, and pepper in a large pot. Cover and boil until vegetables are soft, approximately 25 minutes.

Remove from heat and pour a quarter of the soup mixture into a blender. Blend until smooth. Transfer to a large bowl. Repeat the blending process until all the soup mixture is pureed.

Return mixture from the bowl to the pot. Stir in milk and lemon juice. Heat through, then remove from heat.

Add cheese, stirring until cheese is melted and well blended. Season with additional salt to taste.

Yields 6–8 servings.

"My wife has a pot of potato stew simmerin'."

"Potato?" Mrs. Brown and the vicar both gasped, turning wide-eyed looks of concern on Mariposa.

She knew her part. Blast Jason for that. She buried her face in his jacket and did her best to appear entirely undone at the thought of potatoes being chopped and boiled. And, blast him, she could feel Jason shake as he fought down a chuckle . . .

She raised wide, puppy-dog eyes up to him and, just loudly enough for their travelling companions to hear, asked with a tell-tale break in her voice, "You wouldn't eat the sweet, darlin' potatoes in front of me, would you?"

A Fine Gentleman
Sarah M. Eden

Potato Stew

6 slices of bacon, cut to bite-size pieces
1 large onion, chopped
3–4 green onions, sliced
1½ tablespoons flour
1–2 bay leaves
1 teaspoon dried thyme
¼ cup apple cider vinegar
3 pounds potatoes, peeled and chopped
¼ teaspoon ground black pepper
3 cups chicken broth

In a dutch oven or stockpot, cook the bacon until crisp. Add both types of onion and cook for 3–4 minutes. Add flour, bay leaves, and thyme. Stir.

Increase the heat to high. Pour in vinegar and stir, dislodging any browned bits from the bottom of the dutch oven or stockpot. Cook for 1–2 minutes, until liquid reduces by about half.

Add potatoes, black pepper, and chicken broth. Bring to a boil. Cover, reduce heat to medium-low, and simmer 50–60 minutes. Remove bay leaves before serving. Serve hot.

Yields 4–6 servings.

"Very true," Kendra agreed as she put some water in a pot and started adding the ingredients for her favorite soup. She put everything on to simmer as Charlie crossed back to the kitchen.

He motioned to the stove and asked, "So what's for dinner?"

"Cheddar chowder."

"I don't know that I've ever had that before, but right now, anything hot sounds good."

Obsession
Traci Hunter Abramson

Cheddar Chowder

2 medium potatoes, cubed
1 medium carrot, sliced
1 stalk celery, sliced
1 teaspoon salt
½ teaspoon seasoned salt
¼ teaspoon pepper
1 teaspoon chicken bouillon
2 cups water
¼ cup flour
2 cups milk, divided
8 ounces cheddar cheese, finely shredded

In a large saucepan, combine potatoes, carrot, celery, salt, seasoned salt, pepper, chicken bouillon, and water. Bring to a boil, and then reduce to medium-low heat. Cover and simmer for 15 minutes. Potatoes should be tender. Do not drain.

Combine flour with ¼ cup milk in a small bowl. Add to vegetables, stirring constantly until thickened. Add cheese and remaining milk. Heat until cheese is melted.

Yields 4 servings.

"Cawl," she said, pointing to the bowl.

It was some kind of soup filled with chunks of meat, leeks, and carrots, and it proved to be the best-tasting food Edmund had eaten in a long time.

For Castle and Crown
Sian Ann Bessey

Welsh Cawl

1 pound stewing beef
1 tablespoon vegetable or canola oil
7 cups water
4 teaspoons beef boullion
1 large onion, chopped
1 large carrot, peeled and sliced
1 rutabaga, peeled and cubed
1 parsnip, peeled and sliced
3 medium potatoes, peeled and cubed (I prefer Yukon Gold or reds)
2 leeks, sliced
1 small head cabbage, sliced
¼ teaspoon pepper
2 teaspoons salt

In a frying pan, brown stewing beef in oil.

In a slow cooker, dissolve bouillon in water. Add the browned beef, all the vegetables, and seasonings.

Cook on high for 4 hours or low for 8 hours.

Yields 6–8 servings.

Sophie's footsteps took her to tables laden with food. Some of it she recognized—cakes and fried chicken and tarts—other things were new to her. She suspected those unfamiliar things were offerings from the Irish families, food they'd eaten in their homeland that was not common in America.

"You are welcome to anything that strikes your fancy," Eliza O'Connor said, having come to stand next to her. "Everyone brings something, so no one is burdened by it. And everyone eats their fill."

She struggled to imagine some of the people she knew in Baltimore making such an offering out of sheer kindness. Food at their gatherings was meant to impress, and few of them would be impressed by a pot of bean soup.

Choices of the Heart
Sarah M. Eden

Bean Soup

1 pound ground beef
1 small onion, minced
3 cans pinto or kidney beans (or approximately a quart of cooked beans)
1 can Rotel mild tomatoes

In a large saucepan, sauté ground beef and minced onion together until beef is cooked through. Stir in beans (with liquid) and can of tomatoes. Bring to a simmer. Serve hot.

Yields 4 servings.

Nolan retrieved two bowls from a cabinet and poured cream of mushroom soup into both. He set one bowl in front of Elle and the other at his spot.

“This smells amazing. I can’t believe you made this from scratch.”

“Mushrooms are in season right now. In this area, it’s always easiest to adjust the menu to what is fresh.”

“Yeah, but not a lot of people living on their own cook like this,” Elle said.

On the Run
Traci Hunter Abramson

Nolan's Cream of Mushroom Soup

4 tablespoons butter
1 onion, diced
2 cloves garlic, minced
1 tablespoon vegetable oil
¾ pound fresh mushrooms, sliced
½ teaspoon dried thyme
3 tablespoons flour
2 cups beef broth
1 teaspoon instant chicken bouillon
½ teaspoon salt
⅛ teaspoon pepper
½ cup heavy cream

Melt butter in a medium-sized pot over medium heat. Sauté onion for 3 minutes until softened. Add garlic and cook for 1 minute. Add oil, mushrooms, and thyme. Cook for approximately 7 minutes or until mushrooms are soft. Sprinkle mushrooms with flour and mix well. Add beef broth and bring to a boil. Stir in chicken bouillon, salt, and pepper. Reduce heat to medium-low. Simmer for 10 minutes or until thickened, stirring occasionally. Stir in cream and allow to gently simmer for 1–2 minutes, stirring constantly.

Yields 4 servings.

When Ellie and Austin rejoined the others a while later, Dave immediately slid over and made room for them around the coffee table. Ricky gave Ellie a welcoming smile, and Nina passed them both bowls of soup.

You Came for Me
Sian Ann Bessey

Butternut Squash Soup

4 cups chicken broth
2 medium yams, peeled and cubed
2 medium potatoes, peeled and cubed
2 medium butternut squash, peeled, seeded, and cubed
1 medium onion, peeled and cubed
1 teaspoon dry mustard
½ tablespoon coriander
¾ tablespoon basil
1 (13.5-ounce) can coconut milk
Salt and pepper to taste

In a large pot, combine broth, yams, potatoes, butternut squash, onion, mustard, coriander, and basil. Bring to a boil. Cook on medium heat until tender. Remove from heat.

Place a quarter of the soup in a blender. Blend and pour into a large bowl. Repeat blending process until all the soup is pureed.

Return soup to the pot and add coconut milk. Heat through. Add salt and pepper to taste.

Yields 6–8 servings.

"I believe you have read my wife's thoughts, Lady Devereaux," the duke said between bites. "Pea soup is the first dish she ever had upon arriving in England. It is a particular favorite and one she always eats with great pleasure."

Glimmer of Hope
Sarah M. Eden

Pea Soup

1 (16-ounce) bag of dried split peas
1½ pound slice of bone-in ham
8 cups cold water
1 teaspoon instant chicken bouillon
1 medium onion, chopped
½ teaspoon seasoned salt
¼ teaspoon salt
¼ teaspoon pepper
¼ teaspoon marjoram, crushed
⅛ teaspoon garlic powder

Rinse split peas. Chop ham, reserving bone. In a large pot, combine water, rinsed peas, ham, and ham bone. Add remaining ingredients. Bring to a boil, and then reduce to low heat. Cover and simmer for 90 minutes. Remove bone before serving.

Yields 8–10 servings.

"You know, for someone who is allergic to so many fruits and vegetables, you eat a lot of salad."

"I like salad, and it's something I can't order in restaurants because there always seems to be something in them that I can't have." Elle put some plastic wrap over the top of the salad bowl and put it in the refrigerator.

On the Run
Traci Hunter Abramson

It-Won't-Kill-Me Salad

6 cups torn spinach or favorite greens
Raspberry vinaigrette, as desired
½ cup dried cranberries
½ cup walnuts, chopped
½ cup feta cheese, crumbled

Toss greens with desired amount of dressing. Top with cranberries, walnuts, and feta cheese.

Yields 4–6 servings.

The table was already set for two, and Kendra could see why she hadn't heard him in the back part of the house for so long. He had clearly been busy in the kitchen. A simple white tablecloth covered the ugly kitchen table, and dinner rolls were nestled in a small bowl next to a larger bowl of broccoli salad.

Obsession
Traci Hunter Abramson

Broccoli Salad

Dressing:
1½ cups mayonnaise
½ cup sour cream
⅓ cup sugar
3 tablespoons apple cider vinegar
½ teaspoon salt
¼ teaspoon pepper

Salad base:
8 cups broccoli florets, cut into bite-size pieces
⅔ cup bacon, cooked and crumbled
½ cup red onion, diced
⅔ cup dried cranberries
⅓ cup sunflower seeds
1 cup cheddar cheese, thickly shredded

For the dressing:
Thoroughly mix the ingredients in a medium bowl. Set aside.

For the salad base:
In a large bowl, combine broccoli, bacon, onion, cranberries, and sunflower seeds. Mix in dressing until vegetables are thoroughly coated. Gently stir in shredded cheese.

Yields 8 servings.

"I grew up on a potato farm in Idaho. Potato harvest was such a big operation that they closed schools for a couple of weeks so the children could go work in the fields. We usually had a really good crop of big baking potatoes. But I must say, they never tasted like these."

Forgotten Notes
Sian Ann Bessey

Potato Salad

6 medium potatoes
1 cup mayonnaise
1 tablespoon apple cider vinegar
1 tablespoon sugar
½ tablespoon yellow mustard
1 teaspoon salt
½ teaspoon garlic powder
¼ teaspoon pepper
3 celery ribs, sliced thin
4 hard-boiled eggs, peeled and chopped
Small bunch fresh chives, chopped
Paprika (optional)

Peel, cube, and boil potatoes in salted water until just soft enough to be pierced with a fork. Place in a large bowl and cool.

In a separate bowl, blend mayonnaise, vinegar, sugar, mustard, salt, garlic powder, and pepper. Add to potatoes. Mix well.

Stir in celery, eggs, and chives. Transfer to a serving bowl. Garnish with paprika if desired.

Yields 8–10 servings.

This recipe might as well be called "Mom is on a Deadline Pasta Salad." I make this a lot when time is short. It comes together quickly, is light but filling, and it's simple enough that as they've grown up, my children have learned to make it themselves. So, while it doesn't feature in any of my books, it is the reason a lot of them got finished.

Sarah M. Eden

Spinach, Tomato, and Chicken Pasta Salad

5 ounces bowtie pasta
1½ tablespoons extra-virgin olive oil, divided
½ tablespoon minced garlic, divided
8 ounces spinach, torn into bite-size pieces, divided
¼ teaspoon salt, divided
¼ teaspoon pepper, divided
½ pint cherry tomatoes, halved
4 ounces cooked chicken, shredded
⅛ cup parmesan cheese, shredded

Cook pasta according to package directions. Drain and transfer to a large bowl and set aside.

Heat ½ tablespoon oil in a skillet over medium heat. Add ¼ tablespoon garlic and cook for 30 seconds. Add 4 ounces of spinach and ⅛ teaspoon each of salt and pepper. Sauté 1 minute or until spinach wilts. Add remaining spinach and cook until wilted. Transfer the contents of the skillet into the bowl with the pasta.

Add remaining 1 tablespoon oil and ¼ tablespoon garlic to the skillet. Cook for 30 seconds. Add tomatoes and remaining ⅛ teaspoon each of salt and pepper. Cook 1–2 minutes or until tomatoes release their juices. Add to the bowl with pasta and spinach.

Add chicken and parmesan to the bowl. Toss until well mixed.

Yields 4 servings.

Clearly pleased with how well his surprise had been received, he retrieved a bowl from inside the picnic basket. "I hope shrimp pasta salad is okay. It's one of the few side dishes I know how to make that I can do ahead of time."

"It sounds wonderful."

Chance for Home
Traci Hunter Abramson

Shrimp Pasta Salad

8 ounces small-shell or favorite pasta
8 ounces cooked shrimp
1 cup imitation crab meat, flake style (optional)
2 stalks celery, chopped
½ cup onion, chopped
½ cup ketchup
1 cup mayonnaise
¼ teaspoon Old Bay seasoning

Cook pasta according to package directions. Drain and rinse with cold water. Transfer pasta to a large bowl. Add remaining ingredients and mix well.

Cover and refrigerate for at least two hours. Ideally, this is best made the day before serving.

Yields 4–6 servings.

"I'm going to make a sandwich." She looked from Pete to Tara. "Do either of you want one?"

Pete stared at her for a moment, apparently considering her offer. "Tell you what. If you make me lunch, I might consider letting you practice here this afternoon."

"Go for the chicken salad," Tara suggested, already pulling ingredients out of the refrigerator.

CJ looked over at her and motioned at the groceries Tara had lined up on the counter. "Are you going to help, or do you want to go see who else is hungry?"

"I'll check on the guys."

The Deep End
Traci Hunter Abramson

CJ's Chicken Salad

4 cups cooked chicken, diced
8 ounces cream cheese, softened
½ cup mayonnaise
1 teaspoon seasoned salt
½ cup walnuts, chopped
½ cup celery, chopped
¼ cup diced red onion
1 cup seedless grapes, halved or quartered (optional)

In a large bowl, combine chicken, cream cheese, mayonnaise, and seasoned salt. Gently stir in walnuts, celery, onion, and grapes, if desired. Cover and chill until ready to serve.

Yields 6 servings.

"I've had your colcannon, Maura," he said. "Simply ply them with that, and they'll be singing your praises all evening."

"If nothing else, their mouths will be too full to wage any complaints," she answered dryly.

He nodded toward the door. "Face 'em down. You've bearded fiercer lions."

"Fiercer than you know," she whispered.

"I've no doubt."

Long Journey Home
Sarah M. Eden

Colcannon

1 pound cabbage, washed and shredded
1 pound potatoes, peeled and cut into quarters
1 large leek, trimmed and chopped
½ cup half-and-half
Salt
Black pepper
Pinch of mace or nutmeg
4 ounces melted butter

Preheat oven to 350°F.

In separate saucepans, boil the cabbage and potatoes until cooked. Drain well. Set cabbage aside. Place potatoes in a large mixing bowl and place in the refrigerator.

Add chopped leek and half-and-half to a pan and simmer together for 5–10 minutes.

Remove potatoes from the refrigerator. Add leek and half-and-half mixture. Mash together. Add cabbage, salt, pepper, and mace or nutmeg. Stir until well combined. Turn out into a deep, oven-safe serving dish and place in preheated oven for approximately 10 minutes or until heated through, covering with kitchen foil to prevent browning, if necessary.

Before serving, make a well in the center of the mixture and pour in the melted butter.

Yields 4–6 servings.

Three kartoffelpuffer later, Lars thought he might live to see another day after all.

"It's official," he said. "These are the best potato pancakes I've ever had."

The Danger with Diamonds
Traci Hunter Abramson and Sian Ann Bessey

Christmas Market Kartoffelpuffer (Potato Pancakes)

2½ pounds potatoes, peeled and grated
1 onion, finely chopped
2 large eggs, beaten
½ cup flour
1½ teaspoons salt
¼ teaspoon pepper
Vegetable or canola oil for frying

Rinse the grated raw potato in a sieve. Place on a clean dish towel and squeeze out the excess water.

Mix potato, onion, eggs, flour, salt, and pepper in a large bowl.

Heat a few tablespoons of oil in a large frying pan and place ⅓ to ½ cup of the mixture in the hot pan. Flatten mixture with a spatula. Fry pancake until the edges begin to brown, then flip and cook until both sides are golden.

Place potato pancakes on a plate covered with a paper towel. Serve immediately.

Can be eaten sweet with fruit and powdered sugar or savory with meat and gravy or ketchup.

Yields approximately 8 kartoffelpuffer.

He sampled a bite of the rice with caramelized onions, enjoying the hint of sweet that mixed with the spices. "Where did you learn to cook like this?"

"Nannies are expected to do a lot more than just watch children."

Deep Cover
Traci Hunter Abramson

Rice with Caramelized Onions

1 cup white rice
2¼ cups water
2 teaspoons chicken bouillon
3 tablespoons butter
1 cup sweet onion, thinly sliced
¼ teaspoon garlic powder
1 tablespoon brown sugar

Combine rice, water, and chicken bouillon in a medium saucepan. Bring to a boil. Reduce heat to low, cover, and cook for 15 minutes. Remove from heat, and leave covered for at least 5 minutes.

Meanwhile, melt butter in a medium skillet. Add onion and sauté until lightly browned. Add garlic powder and brown sugar. Cook for 3 minutes, stirring frequently.

Add rice to skillet and mix thoroughly with onions. Serve.

Yields 4 servings.

"How is it you're wanting to prepare your vegetables?"

"Any way at all, really. I haven't the first idea how to go about any of it."

"Easiest is roasting them. You poke 'em a time or two with a fork, then set them amongst the coals. That'll take a bit of time, though."
She nodded, committing the simple instructions to memory. "What if I don't have a great deal of time?"

"Meaning, what if you put off your meal preparation until suppertime and have nothing to eat though you're hungry enough to have a go at the vegetables raw?"

She shrugged a single shoulder. "I suppose that is one possible scenario."

"Then there's but one thing to do."

She was intrigued. "What is that?"

He motioned with his chin toward the chair near his fire. "Same thing you did last night."

"I can't take more food off your table, Mr. McCormick."

"Fair enough." He held out his hand. "You can trade me your potato for a bowl of soup."

Ashes on the Moor
Sarah M. Eden

Oven-Roasted Vegetables

2 tablespoons extra-virgin olive oil
1 teaspoon chipotle & garlic seasoning*
2 cups raw broccoli, chopped
2 cups raw cauliflower, chopped

*Other seasoning mixes can be used, though the amount may need to be adjusted to achieve desired taste

Preheat oven to 425°F.

In a small bowl, mix oil and seasoning. Place vegetables in a gallon-size ziplock bag. Pour oil mixture over vegetables. Seal bag and shake to coat vegetables.

Spread out vegetables on a parchment-paper-lined baking sheet. Bake in the preheated oven for 12–15 minutes, flipping vegetables over at the halfway point.

Yields approximately 6 servings.

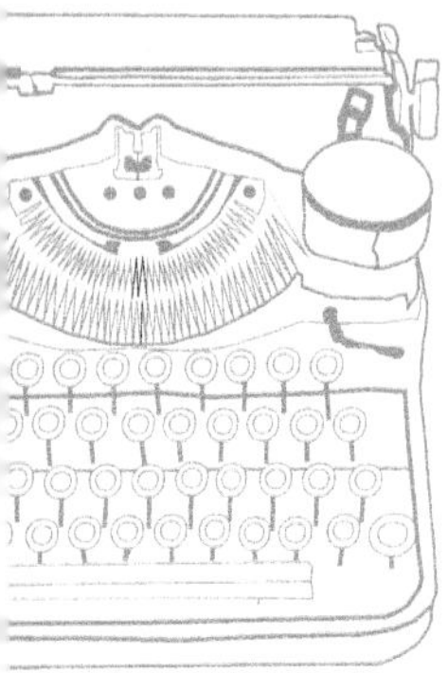

She wasn't sure exactly what she expected, but when she saw the simple meal Katherine had prepared—meatloaf and mashed potatoes—she was pleasantly surprised. She thought that a senator would expect fancier fare than this. Then again, she supposed she would have expected the Whitmores to keep a household staff rather than to see Katherine fixing her own meals.

Backlash
Traci Hunter Abramson

Garlic Mashed Potatoes

5–6 medium potatoes, peeled and quartered
1 (8-ounce) package cream cheese
1 cup butter or margarine
1 teaspoon garlic salt
1 teaspoon seasoned salt
½ cup sour cream

Boil potatoes in salted water until tender (about 20 minutes). Drain.

Blend potatoes, cream cheese, butter or margarine, garlic salt, and seasoned salt with an electric mixer on low until blended. Add sour cream, increase speed to medium-high, and mix until potatoes are smooth and creamy.

Yields 8 servings.

Roast beef. Ham in a raisin sauce. Boiled potatoes in cream. Brussels sprouts and chestnuts. All simple dishes but traditional favorites. ...

Lord Percival turned his attention to Miranda. "These potatoes are delicious. I have always appreciated a good boiled potato."

"As have I," Miranda answered. The compliment was more appreciated than he likely realized. "And this cream sauce is a particular specialty of Cook's."

"It is excellent." Lord Percival punctuated his declaration by returning his attention to savoring the potatoes.

Glimmer of Hope
Sarah M. Eden

*"Boiled potatoes in cream" was a common way of describing *gratin dauphinois*, a French dish that would come to be known by many names, including "potatoes au gratin."

Cheesy Dill Au Gratin Potatoes

3 tablespoons butter
3 tablespoons cornstarch
1 cup buttermilk
2 cups milk

2 tablespoons mayonnaise
½ teaspoon salt
¾ teaspoon dried dill
½ teaspoon garlic powder
½ teaspoon pepper
2½ pounds potatoes, peeled and thinly sliced
¼ cup chopped onion
¼ cup chopped chives, divided
2 cups shredded cheddar cheese, divided

Preheat oven to 375°F. Lightly grease a 9 x 13-inch pan.

In a saucepan, melt the butter. Stir in the cornstarch and whisk until the mixture is smooth and bubbling. Add the buttermilk, milk, mayonnaise, salt, dill, garlic powder, and pepper. Continue whisking until the mixture comes to a boil and thickens. Set aside.

Layer half the potatoes into the bottom of the prepared pan. Top potatoes with chopped onions, half the chives, and half the cheese. Pour half the sauce over the potatoes. Top with the remaining potatoes, followed by remaining sauce and cheese.

Bake uncovered for 55–60 minutes or until the potatoes are easily pierced with a fork. Sprinkle with remaining chopped chives, if desired. Let sit for 10 minutes before serving (this allows the sauce to thicken).

Yields 6–8 servings.

Annie began serving up a meal of roast lamb, mint sauce, mashed potatoes, gravy, and vegetables. It smelled wonderful. After taking a couple of mouthfuls, Brian groaned. "If you keep feeding me like this, Mrs. Lewis, someone's going to have to roll me home!"

Forgotten Notes
Sian Ann Bessey

Welsh Mint Sauce

¼ cup mint leaves, finely chopped
¼ cup boiling water
2 tablespoons cider vinegar
2 tablespoons sugar
¼ teaspoon salt

Place mint leaves in a small bowl or jug. Stir in water, vinegar, sugar, and salt until sugar is dissolved. Cover and let sit for 20 minutes. Serve with roast lamb.

Yields approximately ½ cup mint sauce.

Roast beef. Ham in a raisin sauce. Boiled potatoes in cream. Brussels sprouts and chestnuts. All simple dishes but traditional favorites. That, Miranda had decided, would be the theme for her meal. The food, though enjoyable and filling and satisfying, would not draw undue attention to itself. Dinner would be about the company and the conversation.

With satisfaction, Miranda listened as the guests joined in lively discussions and shared entertaining anecdotes. The menu might not be long remembered, but that night would solidify friendships and provide an evening's enjoyment.

Glimmer of Hope
Sarah M. Eden

Raisin Sauce for Ham

an adaptation of a recipe from 1803

½ cup brown sugar
2 tablespoons cornstarch
1 teaspoon dry mustard
1 cup water
⅛ cup apple cider vinegar
¾ cup golden raisins
2 tablespoons butter

Whisk brown sugar, cornstarch, and mustard powder together in a saucepan. Whisk in water and vinegar. Blend well. Heat on medium-high until the sauce thickens.

Add raisins and butter. Stir well. If the sauce is too thick, add a tablespoon of boiling water and stir to fully incorporate. Repeat as needed to reach desired consistency.

Serve warm over cooked ham.

Yields 1–1½ cups sauce.

MAIN DISHES

Charlotte spooned the marinade over the flank steak, her mind still on that moment in the woods with Jake. For the first time in her life, she found herself faced with hopes and dreams for a home and family, dreams she had never taken much time to consider before, dreams she was afraid to explore now.

Failsafe
Traci Hunter Abramson

Charlotte's Flank Steak

1 cup oil
¼ cup vinegar
1 teaspoon garlic salt
½ cup onion, chopped
Flank steak (approximately 1½ pounds)

Prepare marinade by mixing oil, vinegar, garlic salt, and chopped onion. Marinate the flank steak for 24 hours, turning occasionally.

Grill to desired doneness. Slice and serve.

Though this steak is best when grilled, it can also be broiled.

Yields 4–8 servings.

He pulled open his refrigerator door and stared at the contents—chicken salad, leftover meat-loaf, and a few slices of Steak Diane. He chose the steak and put it in the microwave to heat.

Chance for Home
Traci Hunter Abramson

Steak Diane

2–3 pounds sirloin steak, sliced ¼-inch thick
Dry mustard
Salt
6 tablespoons butter or margarine, divided, plus more for frying
2 tablespoons dried chives
6 tablespoons lemon juice
2 tablespoons Worcestershire sauce

Rub steak with dry mustard and salt and tenderize on each side with a meat mallet. Melt 2 tablespoons butter or margarine in saucepan. Fry steak in butter, about 2 minutes on each side, adding more butter as needed.

Transfer steak to serving dish. Cover to keep warm.

Add to saucepan 4 tablespoons butter or margarine, chives, lemon juice, and Worcestershire sauce. Bring to a boil. Pour over steak. Serve hot.

Yields 4–6 servings.

Mrs. Dalton nodded. "If you're to have an adventure, you'd best eat something first. I've made meat pies."

"Meat pies? You're a saint, Mrs. Dalton." [Harold's] stomach rumbled loudly, agreeing with his assessment.

"I know well your love of meat pies. If I ever needed to bribe you to do something, I'd bake dozens and dozens of them."

"And I would accept."

The Heart of a Vicar
Sarah M. Eden

Easy Hand Pies

For the shell:
2 uncooked pie crusts, homemade or store-bought (if frozen, thaw before using)
Egg whites for brushing

For the filling:
This can be almost anything you fancy, it just needs to be cooked already and have some moisture content. Ideas include . . .

- taco-seasoned ground beef and refried beans
- bite-size potatoes with shredded beef and a small amount of gravy
- leftover shredded chicken from a previous meal
- a can of chunky beef stew or chicken dumpling soup, strained so most of the liquid is out

Heat oven to 425°F.

Roll out pie crusts to approximately 9 inches in diameter. Cut into pizza-shaped wedges (6 per crust for smaller pies, 4 per crust for bigger ones).

Put a couple spoonfuls of filling in the middle of one pie crust triangle. Use another similar-sized triangle as the top and press the edges all around to seal it. (Wetting your fingers with a little water can help with this.) If the pastry is ripping where the filling is, there's too much filling. Repeat until all pie-crust triangles have been used.

Poke each pie twice on the top with a fork to allow venting. Brush the tops and edges of each hand pie with egg whites.

Put pies on a foil- or parchment-lined baking sheet at least an inch apart and bake for 9–12 minutes or until golden brown.

Yields 6 smaller hand pies or 4 larger ones.

Marit watched the man behind the counter ladle thick, steaming goulash into a bread bowl. It looked so good—and so hot.

The Danger with Diamonds
Traci Hunter Abramson and Sian Ann Bessey

Hungarian Goulash

1 large onion, chopped
1 tablespoon olive oil
1½ tablespoons sweet paprika
1 pound stewing beef, cubed
1 (15-ounce) can beef broth
1 (15-ounce) can diced tomatoes
4 carrots, peeled and sliced
3 small red potatoes, cubed
1 teaspoon salt
¼ teaspoon pepper

In a frying pan, sauté onion in oil until translucent. Stir in paprika. Add beef and cook until lightly browned. Transfer to slow cooker. Add beef broth, tomatoes, carrots, potatoes, and seasonings. Cook on high for 4 hours or on low for 6–8 hours.

Yields 4–6 servings.

He preferred his own personal concerns remain personal, so he'd not press himself into hers. "Take up a knife. You'll be chopping the carrots."

"Is there any particular trick to it?"

"Only one." He pushed the pile of carrots closer to her. "Aim for the vegetables, not your fingers."

Ashes on the Moor
Sarah M. Eden

Kelsey walked to the countertop, where a pot roast was simmering in the slow cooker. After getting a taste of American food with Noah the other night, she found she wanted to reacquaint herself with some more of her old favorites.

Deep Cover
Traci Hunter Abramson

Pot Roast

3 potatoes, peeled and thinly sliced
3 medium carrots, peeled and sliced
1 onion, peeled and sliced
3 pounds pot roast
1 teaspoon seasoned salt
1 teaspoon salt
¼ teaspoon thyme
¼ teaspoon pepper
½ cup water

Layer vegetables in the bottom of a slow cooker. Add roast, seasonings, and water. Cover and cook on low for approximately 10 hours or on high for approximately 5 hours. Serve hot.

Yields 6–8 servings.

I have no doubt you have been working long hours in the cart shed, so I am sending you some pasties—you did say they were your favorite—as I am equally sure you are neglecting your meals.

An Alleged Rogue
Sian Ann Bessey

Cornish Pasties

Pastry:
2½ cups flour
1 teaspoon salt
1 cup shortening
1 egg, beaten
1 tablespoon vinegar
¼ cup cold water

Filling:
1 large yellow potato, peeled and diced
1 parsnip, peeled and diced
1 large carrot, peeled and diced
1 onion, chopped
Salt and pepper to taste
1 pound stewing beef, cut into small cubes
Butter (approximately 4 tablespoons)
Flour (approximately 2 tablespoons)
1 egg, beaten

For the pastry:
In a large bowl, mix dry ingredients. Cut in shortening with a pastry cutter or two knives or rub in with fingers until mixture resembles crumbs. Form a well in the center. Fill with beaten egg, vinegar, and water. Blend with a fork until the mixture comes together to form a dough. Wrap dough in plastic wrap and chill while preparing the filling ingredients.

Preheat the oven to 350°F.

Divide the pastry into 6 portions. Roll each portion into a circle about ⅛-inch thick. Use an 8-inch-diameter plate as a guide to cut a circle out of each one.

For the filling:
Using ⅙ of each of the vegetables and the meat, place a layer of potatoes in a line down the center of one pastry circle, leaving about ¾-inch space at the top and bottom edges. Sprinkle with salt and pepper. Add a layer of parsnips, carrots, and onions, followed by another sprinkle of salt and pepper. Top with a layer of the cubed beef. Place a couple of pats of butter (approximately 1 teaspoon each) on the beef and sprinkle with approximately 1 teaspoon flour.

Gently bring the sides of the pastry up and seal the pasty down the middle. Turn the pasty on its side and crimp the edges together to form a sealed semi-circle. Repeat this process for each pasty, and set them on a baking sheet lined with parchment paper. Use a sharp knife to cut 2 or 3 half-inch slits in the center of each pasty. Brush with beaten egg.

Bake for 40–50 minutes until golden in color. Remove from the oven and allow to sit for 10 minutes before serving.

Yields 6 pasties.

"Are you sure about this?" Amy asked reluctantly.

"Absolutely." Riley tapped the cookbook in front of her and handed Amy a spoon. "Meatloaf is easy to make, and if the measurements don't work out exactly, it won't really matter."

Lockdown
Traci Hunter Abramson

Even-Amy-Can-Make-It Meatloaf

1 pound ground beef or ground turkey
1 egg
¼ cup onion, chopped
½ cup celery, chopped
½ cup bread crumbs
1 cup sour cream
¼ cup ketchup or barbecue sauce
1 teaspoon salt
½ teaspoon seasoned salt
¼ teaspoon pepper
2 ounces cheddar cheese, sliced

Preheat oven to 350°F.

Combine all ingredients except cheese. Mix well.

Pour into a loaf pan and bake for 40 minutes. Place slices of cheese on top of meatloaf. Bake for an additional 5 minutes or until cheese is melted.

Yields 4–6 servings.

Kelsey stood at the stove, a spatula in her hand. Her hair was pulled back in a messy knot at the nape of her neck, and she was wearing the bib apron Kelsey's father had given [Noah] that read *Consider your words carefully. I shoot people for a living.* A plate of Indian fry bread sat on the counter alongside a platter piled high with meat and vegetables on skewers that she had apparently just taken off the grill.

Deep Cover
Traci Hunter Abramson

Grilled Beef and Scallop Kabobs

Beef marinade:
1 cup olive oil
½ cup soy sauce
⅓ cup lemon juice
¼ cup Worcestershire sauce
¼ cup yellow mustard
2 cloves garlic, minced
1 teaspoon pepper

Kabobs:
½ pound 1-inch-thick steak, cut into one-inch cubes
½ pound scallops

8 cherry tomatoes
8 pearl onions
8 whole mushrooms
½ cup pineapple chunks
4 skewers

Lemon juice mixture (for brushing on skewers):
2 tablespoons vegetable oil
2 teaspoons soy sauce
2 tablespoons lemon juice
½ teaspoon Old Bay seasoning

Combine all ingredients for marinade in a gallon-sized ziplock bag. Add steak cubes to mixture and marinate in the refrigerator for 4–24 hours.

Before assembly: In a small bowl, combine oil, soy sauce, lemon juice, and Old Bay seasoning. Marinate scallops in lemon juice mixture in refrigerator for 10–15 minutes.

Assemble kabobs by alternating marinated beef, scallops, tomatoes, onions, mushrooms, and pineapple on each of the 4 skewers.

Brush lemon juice mixture over kabobs.

To grill:
Grill kabobs over medium coals for 10–15 minutes or until scallops are opaque. Brush kabobs frequently with lemon mixture.

To broil:
Baste kabobs with lemon mixture. Broil for about 8 minutes or until scallops are opaque.

Yields 4 kabobs.

He'd not have guessed when they'd first met that she'd be one for playful banter. Truth be told, he'd not known that about himself before Evangeline had arrived in his life. "I'd not object to it, though it'd depend on how much you're meaning to charge me for that bit of information."

"Are you saying that I could make my fortune on this?"

"Well, I'd have to pay you in coddle."

Her eyes pulled wide. "Cuddle?"

He laughed long and hard. "Good heavens, woman." His attempt at controlling his mirth only led to a deeper fit of laughter. "Coddle. Not cuddle. It's a stew from Dublin."

She pressed her hands over her mouth, color splotching her cheeks. He likely should've stopped laughing then, but saints above, the particular nature of the misunderstanding coupled with her look of shock was simply too much.

"Stop it." Her eyes danced, a sure sign she was not truly humiliated by the error. "It was an honest mistake."

"What was that you said? A hopeful mistake?"

She nudged him with her shoulder as she passed. "Hopeful on whose part, Dermot?"

Oh, on his part, to be sure.

Ashes on the Moor
Sarah M. Eden

Dublin Coddle

1 pound ground pork sausage
1 pound thick-cut bacon
1 large onion, sliced
2 pounds potatoes, peeled and quartered
Kosher salt
Black pepper
1 tablespoon fresh parsley, finely chopped
2 cups chicken/beef/vegetable broth

Preheat oven to 300°F.

In a skillet, brown the sausage and bacon. Once fully cooked, chop into bite-size pieces.

Put onions, bacon, sausage, and potatoes in a dutch oven or large casserole dish with a tight lid. Season with salt, pepper, and parsley. Pour broth over the top.

Place the covered dutch oven/casserole dish in the preheated oven and cook for 3 hours. After 2 hours, check liquid levels and add more water/broth if less than an inch of liquid is left in the bottom of the pot.

Yields 6–8 servings.

The back door opened, and Miles walked in carrying a stack of firewood. "Are you talking about me again?"

"Only about your love of pork chops."

"You do make the best."

An Unlikely Pair
Traci Hunter Abramson

Catalina Pork Chops

¼ cup mayonnaise
¼ cup Catalina dressing
1 package instant onion soup mix
½ cup apricot preserves
½ cup pineapple preserves
2½ pounds pork chops

Preheat oven to 325°F.

Combine mayonnaise, dressing, soup mix, and preserves. Place pork chops in a 9 x 13-inch baking dish and spoon mixture evenly over the pork chops.

Bake for 1½ hours. Serve with rice.

Yields 4–6 servings.

No need to make another meal the next day because the leftovers are so good.

Sian Ann Bessey

Deadline-Crunch Cashew Pad Thai

Sauce:
4½ tablespoons soy sauce
7½ tablespoons sugar
3 tablespoons rice vinegar
1½ teaspoons Sriracha sauce
3 tablespoons cashew butter

Pad Thai:
8 ounces flat rice noodles
3 tablespoons olive oil, divided

8 ounces chicken or extra-firm tofu, cubed
3 cloves garlic, minced
1 cup matchstick carrots
1 head of broccoli, cut into small florets
1 red bell pepper, sliced thin
2 eggs, beaten
1 cup fresh bean sprouts
½ cup cashews
3 green onions, sliced
½ cup fresh cilantro, chopped
2 limes, quartered

For the sauce:
Mix the ingredients together in a blender. Set aside.

Cook noodles until just tender. Rinse under cold water. Set aside.

For the Pad Thai:
Heat 1½ tablespoons of oil in a large saucepan or wok over medium-high heat. Add the chicken or tofu. Cook through. Add garlic, carrots, broccoli, and bell pepper. Cook for 3–5 minutes. Push everything to the sides of the pan, add remaining oil, then pour beaten eggs into the center of the pan. Scramble the eggs, breaking them into small pieces with a spatula as they cook. Mix cooked egg with the other ingredients in the pan.

Add noodles, sauce, bean sprouts, and cashews to the pan. Toss to combine. Top with green onions and cilantro.

Serve with lime wedges.

Yields 6–8 servings.

Having a child with a long list of significant food allergies has meant inventing meals that the whole family can enjoy. I threw this one together one day using ingredients I had on hand, and it became an instant favorite. It is now on regular rotation at the Eden house. And it is easy enough to make that the kids quickly learned to prepare it themselves.

Sarah M. Eden

Mock Chicken Alfredo

(Dairy-free, Egg-free, Nut-free, Gluten-free)

6 ounces rice noodles (check packaging for any allergen warnings; this varies between manufacturers)
1 tablespoon extra-virgin olive oil
1 clove of garlic, minced
1 head of broccoli, chopped and steamed
2 cups cooked chicken, shredded or cubed
Salt
Pepper
Apple cider vinegar (optional)

Cook noodles according to package instructions. Drain.

Heat oil in a skillet on medium heat. Add garlic and cook for 1 minute. Add steamed broccoli and chicken. Sauté on medium-low until heated through. Add rice noodles. Stir well.

Add salt and pepper to taste. For extra zing, add a dash or two of apple cider vinegar.

Serve hot.

Yields 4 servings.

"I'm from India originally."

"Ahhh. The land of curry and spice," he said, the simplistic description invoking images of her family gathered together to share a meal of pilau rice and kadai lamb. "Do you know how to make curry chicken?"

Delighted despite her exhaustion, she offered him a warm smile. "Of course. It's one of my favorite foods."

"Maybe one day after you're better, I'll talk you into making that for me. My wife never has been able to get it quite right."

"Is your wife from India?"

"No. New Jersey."

Chances Are
Traci Hunter Abramson

Curry Chicken

2 tablespoons olive oil
2 pounds boneless, skinless chicken breasts or thighs, cubed
1 packet sazón (or 1¼ teaspoons)
1 teaspoon salt
¼ teaspoon pepper
1 cup onion, chopped
3 cloves garlic, minced
2 teaspoons curry powder
1 cup chicken broth, low-sodium
1 (14-ounce) can coconut milk
1 (14.5-ounce) can petite diced tomatoes
1 tablespoon cumin
1 teaspoon turmeric
½ teaspoon ginger

Heat oil in a large skillet. Add chicken, sazon, salt, and pepper. Stir chicken to coat with seasonings. Cook chicken for about 5 minutes or until chicken is no longer pink. Add chopped onion. Stir for approximately 3 minutes or until onion softens. Add garlic and cook for an additional 2–3 minutes. Add curry powder and stir, then add remaining ingredients. Cover and simmer for 15 minutes.

Yields 4–6 servings.

They both chose Tandoori chicken and rice—Ellie because she couldn't wait to have it again and Austin because he said he wanted to try it for the first time.

You Came for Me
Sian Ann Bessey

If this Tikka Masala had been on the menu, I'm pretty sure Ellie and Austin would have chosen it instead.

Sian Ann Bessey

Should-Have-Chosen Chicken Tikka Masala

3 boneless, skinless chicken breasts, cut into bite-size pieces

Marinade:
1 cup plain yogurt
1 tablespoon lemon juice
2 teaspoons cumin
1 teaspoon cinnamon
1 teaspoon garam masala
¼ teaspoon cayenne
¼ teaspoon pepper
1 tablespoon minced fresh ginger
1 teaspoon salt

Sauce:
1 tablespoon butter or olive oil
1 clove garlic, minced
2 teaspoons cumin
2 teaspoons paprika
1 teaspoon garam masala
½ teaspoon chili powder
1 teaspoon salt
1 (8-ounce) can tomato sauce
1 cup heavy cream

Garnish:
¼ cup fresh cilantro, chopped

For the marinade:
In a large bowl, combine yogurt, lemon juice, cumin, cinnamon, garam masala, cayenne, pepper, ginger, and salt. Stir in chicken until well coated. Cover and refrigerate 1 hour or overnight.

Heat a tablespoon of oil in a large frying pan and transfer the chicken pieces to the pan. Cook through and discard remaining marinade.

For the sauce:
Heat butter or oil in a large skillet over medium-low heat. Sauté garlic for 1 minute. Season with cumin, paprika, garam masala, chili powder, and salt. Stir in tomato sauce and cream. Simmer on low heat until sauce thickens, about 20 minutes.

Add cooked chicken to the sauce and simmer for 5 more minutes. Serve over cooked jasmine rice and sprinkle with fresh chopped cilantro.

Yields 4–6 servings.

"The chicken just needs to cook for a few more minutes." Charlie draped her coat over the side of a chair to dry and looked over at her, a sudden look of concern crossing his face. "You aren't a vegetarian, are you?"

A giggle escaped her. "No, I'm not a vegetarian."

Obsession
Traci Hunter Abramson

Charlie's Southwestern Chicken and Rice

2 tablespoons oil
1 medium onion, chopped
1 (14.5-ounce) can diced tomatoes
1 (4-ounce) can diced green chiles
2 cups water
2 teaspoons instant chicken bouillon
¾ cup uncooked white rice
2 cups frozen corn
1 teaspoon chili powder
½ teaspoon salt
¼ teaspoon pepper
⅛ teaspoon garlic powder
4 tablespoons flour
2 teaspoons garlic salt
2 tablespoons paprika
8 chicken thighs and/or drumsticks (2½ to 3 pounds)

Preheat oven to 375°F.

Heat oil in saucepan over medium heat. Sauté onion until tender. Add undrained tomatoes, green chiles, water, bouillon, rice, corn, chili powder, salt, pepper, and garlic powder. Bring to a boil and simmer on low for 3 minutes. Pour mixture into an ungreased 9 x 13-inch baking pan.

Combine flour, garlic salt, and paprika in a 1-gallon plastic bag. Shake to mix. Add chicken a few pieces at a time. Shake to coat. Place chicken pieces on rice mixture. Press lightly into rice. Cover pan tightly with foil. Bake for 60 to 85 minutes or until chicken is tender and juices run clear. Remove foil. Bake an additional 15 minutes uncovered.

Yields 8 servings.

"Noelle, you have to stay too."

"I have a flight, remember?"

"You have a flight on a private jet," Mary replied. "Call the pilot and see if he can move back your departure time. Your driver is welcome to join us for dinner too if he wants."

Noelle wavered, not sure she should take advantage of having access to the royal family's private plane. "I don't know . . ."

"Did I mention I'm making enchiladas for dinner?"

Unable to resist, Noelle smiled. "I guess it can't hurt to make a call."

Royal Brides
Traci Hunter Abramson

Irresistible Chicken Enchiladas

2 (12.5-ounce) cans chicken, drained
8 ounces cream cheese, cubed
1 (4.5-ounce) can diced green chiles
½ teaspoon cumin
⅛ teaspoon garlic powder
12 (6-inch) flour tortillas
1 (10-ounce) can green chile enchilada sauce
½ cup cheddar or cheddar/monterey jack cheese, shredded

Preheat oven to 400°F.

In a medium skillet, combine chicken, cream cheese, green chiles, cumin, and garlic powder. Cook over medium heat until cream cheese is melted and ingredients are well blended. Remove from heat.

Fill each tortilla with 1/12 of the filling. Roll and place seam-side down in a greased 9 x 13-inch baking pan. Cover rolled tortillas with enchilada sauce. Sprinkle cheese evenly over the top. Bake for 15 minutes or until enchiladas are heated through and cheese is melted.

Yields 6 servings.

"You know how to make crepes?"

"Before we're done tonight, you'll know how to make them too."

Not Dead Yet
Traci Hunter Abramson

His gaze dropped to her empty plate. "You didn't have to wait for me."

"I knew you would be back soon." She lifted the cover off a dish. "Patrice sent us chicken-and-mushroom crepes."

"Sounds good."

Royal Heir
Traci Hunter Abramson

Cas's Chicken Crepes

Crepe batter:
½ cup milk
½ cup water
2 large eggs
1 tablespoon butter, melted
1 cup flour

Filling:
2 tablespoons butter
1 medium onion, thinly sliced and quartered
½ pound mushrooms, sliced
1 tablespoon flour
2 cups cooked chicken, shredded
1 cup chicken broth
½ teaspoon salt
¼ teaspoon thyme
⅛ teaspoon garlic powder
⅛ teaspoon pepper
¼ cup heavy cream

Sauce:
1 tablespoon butter
1 tablespoon flour
⅓ cup heavy cream
½ cup chicken broth
¼ teaspoon salt
⅛ teaspoon garlic powder
⅛ teaspoon pepper
1 cup swiss cheese, shredded

Garnish (optional):
Freshly chopped parsley

For the batter:
Mix all ingredients for the crepe batter with an electric mixer. Refrigerate for at least a half hour.

For the filling:
In a medium skillet, melt 2 tablespoons butter and sauté onion for approximately 3 minutes or until onion is soft. Add mushrooms and sauté until vegetables are soft. Sprinkle 1 tablespoon of flour over vegetables and mix. Add chicken, chicken broth, ½ teaspoon salt, thyme, and ⅛ teaspoon each of garlic powder and pepper. Stir in ¼ cup heavy cream. Reduce heat to low and heat through. Set aside.

For the sauce:
Melt 1 tablespoon butter and mix with 1 tablespoon flour. Slowly add ⅓ cup heavy cream. Mix well and heat on low. Slowly add ½ cup chicken broth. Stir in ¼ teaspoon salt and ⅛ teaspoon each of garlic powder and pepper. Add swiss cheese and stir over medium-low heat until cheese is thoroughly melted. Set aside.

To make the crepes:
Heat crepe maker or medium nonstick skillet. Add ¼ cup of batter and either use a crepe spreader or lift the skillet and gently tilt it until the crepe batter spreads evenly over the bottom of the pan.

Cook for about a minute or until the edges start to curl up. Use a spatula or crepe turner to flip over. Cook for an additional minute or until cooked through.

Move cooked crepe to a plate and spread 2–3 tablespoons of filling on one end of the crepe. Roll. Ladle sauce over the top. If desired, garnish with freshly chopped parsley.

Yields 4–6 servings.

Garrett dropped into the seat across from his brother. “Patrice said to tell you she was making you some chicken cordon bleu for dinner.”

“Chicken cordon bleu is your favorite dinner, not mine.”

“Yeah, I know.” Garrett grinned. “What can I say? I can’t help it if Patrice loves me best.”

Royal Secrets
Traci Hunter Abramson

Chicken Cordon Bleu

4 boneless, skinless chicken breast halves
4 slices domestic cooked ham
4 ounces swiss cheese, cut into 4 pieces
1 tablespoon flour
4 tablespoons butter or margarine, divided
¼ pound fresh mushrooms, sliced
½ cup onion, chopped
¾ cup water
1 teaspoon instant chicken bouillon
1 tablespoon fresh parsley, chopped
1 teaspoon fresh chives, snipped
⅓ cup heavy cream

With a meat mallet, flatten each chicken breast to approximately ¼–½-inch thick. Top each chicken breast with a piece of ham and a piece of swiss cheese. Starting at the narrow end of the chicken breast, roll up the chicken breast and ham around the piece of cheese. Use toothpicks to hold each roll together.

Lightly coat each chicken roll with flour. In a large skillet, melt 2 tablespoons of butter or margarine over medium heat. Add chicken rolls and brown on all sides. Remove from pan and set aside.

Melt remaining butter in skillet and add mushrooms and onion. Sauté until tender.

Add water, chicken bouillon, parsley, and chives. Bring to a boil. Return chicken rolls to sauce. Lower heat, cover, and simmer for 30 minutes.

Transfer chicken to serving platter. Bring sauce to a boil and stir in heavy cream. Lower heat and simmer 3 minutes. Pour sauce over chicken rolls. Serve with rice.

Yields 4 servings.

After the blessing was said, Brent's mom dished out the chicken parmesan. Brent eyed it suspiciously, cutting off a small bite to sample.

Pleasantly surprised, he cut off a larger bite, considering. His father didn't make Italian food, and his mother didn't make food period. As he prepared to enjoy the meal before him, he spoke to his mother. "This is really good, Mom. Who made it?"

Amy's eyebrows rose at the subtle insult.

Noticing her expression, Brent explained, "Mom doesn't cook."

"He's right." She nodded and motioned to her husband. "Tom does most of the cooking. I'm much better at dialing for takeout, but today our neighbor down the street cooked for us."

Freefall
Traci Hunter Abramson

Chicken Parmesan

½ cup dry bread crumbs
2 tablespoons parmesan cheese
4 boneless, skinless chicken breast halves
1 egg, beaten
2 tablespoons butter or margarine
2 cups spaghetti sauce
1 cup mozzarella cheese, shredded
8 ounces uncooked pasta (spaghetti, penne rigate, or other favorite)

Combine bread crumbs and parmesan cheese in a bowl. Dip chicken into egg and then coat evenly with bread crumb mixture.

Melt butter or margarine in a large skillet. Place chicken in skillet and cook over medium heat until done and juices run clear (about 5 minutes on each side). Add spaghetti sauce. Cook until spaghetti sauce is heated through. Cover and reduce heat. Simmer for 5 minutes. Top chicken with mozzarella and heat until cheese melts.

Meanwhile, cook pasta according to package directions. Drain and pour into serving dish. Top with chicken and sauce.

Yields 4 servings.

Tonight, they wouldn't have his favorite meal but rather the apricot-glazed salmon Jane's mother had assured him was her favorite.

Tripwire
Traci Hunter Abramson

The dowager dripped soup off her spoon back into the bowl. Though she clearly didn't like the offering, she still sent smiles across the table at each of the guests in turn.

Miranda looked across the table at Carter. He didn't seem to have any objections. Indeed, he and the duchess and Lady Percival were tucking enthusiastically into the cod. Salmon and halibut had been the fish of choice thus far during the house party.

Glimmer of Hope
Sarah M. Eden

Apricot-Glazed Salmon

Glaze:
3 tablespoons butter or margarine
½ cup apricot preserves
1 tablespoon honey
½ teaspoon Old Bay seasoning
¼ teaspoon cardamom
¼ teaspoon salt
⅛ teaspoon pepper

Salmon fillet, approximately 2 pounds
2–3 tablespoons butter or margarine

Preheat oven to 375°F.

For the glaze:
In a small saucepan, melt butter or margarine over low heat and add preserves, honey, Old Bay seasoning, cardamom, salt, and pepper. Stir until well blended.

To prepare salmon:
Line baking tray with aluminum foil. Place salmon fillet on tray. Make ½-inch-deep cuts in salmon about every 2 inches. Cut butter or margarine into narrow slices, about 4 or 5 per tablespoon. Place pats of butter or margarine in the cuts made in the salmon. Brush glaze evenly over salmon, making sure the glaze goes into cuts. Bake in preheated oven for 16–20 minutes or until salmon flakes easily with a fork.

Yields 6 servings.

"*Oui.* I miss my family there. I miss Paris and our country home. I long for a hot bowl of ratatouille on cold days." [Henri's] voice had turned nostalgic. "But England is home to me now. I would not wish to live anywhere else. And I should like a bit of it to call my own."

Lily of the Valley
Sarah M. Eden

Ratatouille

2 tablespoons extra-virgin olive oil, divided
2 cloves garlic, minced
1 eggplant, sliced into bite-size pieces
2 teaspoons dried parsley
1 cup fresh parmesan cheese, grated and divided
Salt and pepper to taste
1 zucchini, sliced into bite-size pieces
1 large red onion, sliced into rings
2 cups fresh mushrooms, sliced
1 yellow bell pepper, sliced
2 large tomatoes, chopped

Preheat oven to 350°F.

Coat bottom and sides of a 9 x 13-inch glass casserole dish with 1 tablespoon oil.

Heat remaining oil in a medium skillet over medium heat. Sauté garlic until lightly golden. Add eggplant and sprinkle with parsley. Sauté 8–10 minutes until eggplant is soft.

Put eggplant mixture in prepared casserole dish. Sprinkle with a little parmesan cheese and salt and pepper. Add zucchini in an even layer on top of eggplant. Sprinkle with a little parmesan cheese and salt and pepper. Continue layering remaining ingredients with parmesan, salt, and pepper sprinkled between each layer.

Bake uncovered in the preheated oven for 45 minutes.

Serve hot.

Yields 4–6 servings.

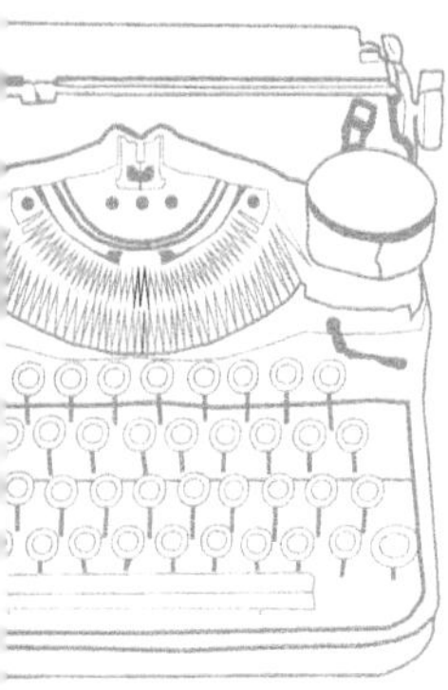

She took her time looking over the menu, though she already knew she wanted arepas con queso.

When the cheese-filled corncakes arrived, she ate slowly, lingering over her meal. After more than an hour, she paid her bill and headed for the elevators.

Drop Zone
Traci Hunter Abramson

Arepas con Queso

½ teaspoon salt
1 cup plus 2 tablespoons warm water
1 cup pre-cooked white cornmeal
2 tablespoons vegetable oil
⅔ cup mozzarella cheese

Dissolve salt in warm water. Mix in cornmeal. Let rise five minutes. Separate dough into five sections and create five patties about a half-inch thick.

Heat oil in skillet. Pan fry patties over medium heat, covered, for 5–6 minutes. Flip arepas over and cook for another 5–6 minutes.

Remove from heat. Cut arepas in half and fill center of each arepa with approximately 2 tablespoons of mozzarella cheese. If desired, return arepas to skillet for a minute to melt cheese completely. Serve hot.

Yields 5 servings.

“That’s fine for you,” Kade said, looking a little frustrated. “But what about my pizza?”

Failsafe
Traci Hunter Abramson

Where's Kade's Pizza?

1¼ cups warm water
1 teaspoon sugar
1 tablespoon yeast
2 tablespoons olive oil
3¼ cups flour
½ teaspoon salt
½ teaspoon italian seasoning
⅛ teaspoon garlic powder
1 teaspoon parmesan cheese, grated (optional)
¾ cup spaghetti, pizza, or alfredo sauce
3 cups mozzarella cheese, shredded and divided

Preheat oven to 400°F.

Combine water, sugar, and yeast in a large bowl. Let sit for 3 minutes. Add oil.

In a medium bowl, mix flour with salt, italian seasoning, garlic powder, and parmesan cheese, if desired. Add to yeast mixture a cup at a time, kneading by hand if necessary. Cover dough and let rise for one hour or until approximately double in size.

Punch down dough and divide in two parts. Roll each half into a 10–12-inch circle on a baking stone or a lightly greased baking sheet. For each pizza, spread ¼–⅓ cup of sauce evenly over dough. Sprinkle 1½ cups of cheese over sauce.

Bake for 17–20 minutes or until crust is lightly golden and cheese is melted.

Yields 2 medium pizzas.

This is my go-to meal when I need comfort food in a hurry. My whole family loves it.

Sian Ann Bessey

Spent-All-Day-Writing Chicken Tetrazzini

8 ounces spaghetti
1 pound chicken tenders, cubed and cooked
3 tablespoons butter
3 tablespoons cornstarch
1 (14.5 ounce) can chicken broth
1 cup milk
Parmesan cheese, grated
Parsley flakes

Preheat oven to 350°F.

Cook spaghetti according to package directions. Drain pasta and place in a greased 9 x 13-inch pan. Cover with cubed, cooked chicken.

Melt butter in a saucepan. Add cornstarch. Mix well and bring to a boil. Add chicken broth and milk. Whisk continually until it comes to a boil. Boil for 1 minute or until it thickens slightly. Pour over chicken and spaghetti.

Sprinkle generously with grated parmesan cheese and parsley flakes. Bake uncovered for 30–35 minutes.

Yields 6–8 servings.

Tip: for an even faster meal, precook the chicken and freeze beforehand or use rotisserie chicken.

"You expect an awful lot for some lasagna," Tristan said, even as he took another bite.

Smoke Screen
Traci Hunter Abramson

Riley's Lasagna

1 pound ground pork or italian sausage
1 pound ground beef
1 clove garlic, minced
3 tablespoons parsley flakes, divided
2½ tablespoons fresh basil or 1 tablespoon dried basil
2½ teaspoons salt, divided
2 (14.5-ounce) cans diced tomatoes with juices
2 (6-ounce) cans tomato paste
8 ounces lasagna noodles
3 cups cottage cheese
2 eggs, beaten
1 cup parmesan cheese
16 ounces mozzarella cheese, shredded

In a large skillet, brown sausage and ground beef. Drain. Stir in garlic, 1 tablespoon parsley flakes, basil, 1½ teaspoons salt, tomatoes, and tomato paste. Bring to boil. Reduce heat, and simmer for 30 minutes.

Meanwhile, cook lasagna noodles according to package directions.

Preheat oven to 375°F.

In a medium bowl, combine cottage cheese, eggs, 1 teaspoon salt, 2 tablespoons parsley flakes, and parmesan cheese.

Cover the bottom of a greased 9 x 13-inch pan with half of the noodles. Cover noodles with half of the sauce, half of the cottage cheese mixture, and half of the mozzarella cheese. Repeat.

Bake for 30 minutes. Let stand 10 minutes before serving.

Yields 6–8 servings.

Quinn fought back a smile. “You don’t see mac and cheese?”

She eyed him over the top of the menu. “Go ahead and mock,” she said. “But if you’d ever tasted my mom’s homemade mac and cheese, that’s what you’d want too.”

The Gem Thief
Sian Ann Bessey

Mrs. Miller's Macaroni and Cheese

12 ounces macaroni, penne, or rotini noodles
½ teaspoon mustard powder
1 cup and 1 teaspoon water
¼ cup butter
1 clove garlic, minced
3 tablespoons cornstarch
3 cups milk
1 teaspoon chicken bouillon
⅛ teaspoon pepper
4 cups sharp cheddar cheese, grated and divided
Salt to taste
Grated parmesan cheese

Preheat oven to 350° F.

Cook noodles as directed on package. Drain and set aside.

Mix mustard powder with 1 teaspoon water to form a paste. In a large saucepan, melt butter. Add mustard paste and minced garlic. Cook for 1 minute. Stir in cornstarch. With a whisk, stir in milk, bouillon, pepper, and remaining 1 cup water. Bring to a boil. Allow to boil for 1 minute. Remove from heat and add 3 cups cheese. Stir until sauce is smooth. Add salt to taste.

Pour cooked noodles into the sauce. Stir to combine and transfer to a greased 9 x 13-inch pan. Cover with approximately 1 cup cheddar cheese and sprinkle liberally with grated parmesan.

Bake uncovered for 20–25 minutes or until golden brown.

Yields 6–8 servings.

"She'll want your beef stroganoff."

Eleanor narrowed her eyes. "Did you suggest that to her?"

"Maybe. I love stroganoff."

Dreams of Gold
Traci Hunter Abramson

Simply Special Stroganoff

3 tablespoons butter or margarine
¼ cup onion, chopped
8 ounces mushrooms, sliced
1 pound ground beef or ground turkey
⅛ teaspoon garlic powder
3½ cups water
4 beef bouillon cubes
2 teaspoons lemon juice
12 ounces uncooked egg noodles
1½ cups sour cream
Paprika

Melt butter in a large skillet. Add onion and mushrooms. Sauté until vegetables are tender. Add ground beef or ground turkey and garlic powder. Cook until meat is browned. Drain.

Return to heat and add water, bouillon cubes, and lemon juice. Simmer uncovered for 5 minutes. Stir in noodles. Cover and cook for an additional 15 minutes or until noodles are tender, stirring occasionally and adding more water if necessary.

Stir in sour cream and heat through without bringing to a boil. Sprinkle with paprika and serve.

Yields 4–6 servings.

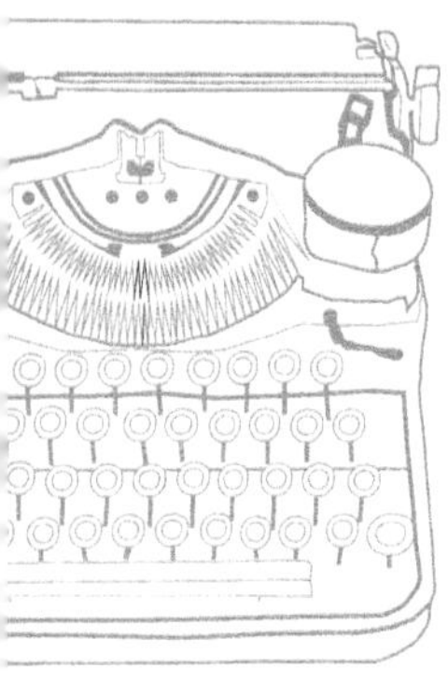

"How about tuna casserole?" Shaye suggested, lining the ingredients up on the counter.

"I thought I was going to cook for you."

"I have a feeling that most of the cooking you do involves dialing the phone."

Undercurrents
Traci Hunter Abramson

Shaye's Tuna Casserole

8 ounces elbow macaroni
1 (10¾-ounce) can condensed cream of mushroom soup
½ cup milk
1 (6-ounce) can tuna, drained
½ cup cooked peas (optional)
1 cup cheddar cheese, shredded

Preheat oven to 325°F.

Cook pasta according to package directions.

Combine cooked macaroni with soup, milk, tuna, and peas, if desired. Pour half of macaroni mixture into a 1½-quart casserole dish. Sprinkle half of the cheese over the mixture. Then add remaining pasta to dish and top with remaining cheese.

Bake for 25 minutes or until heated through.

Yields 4–6 servings.

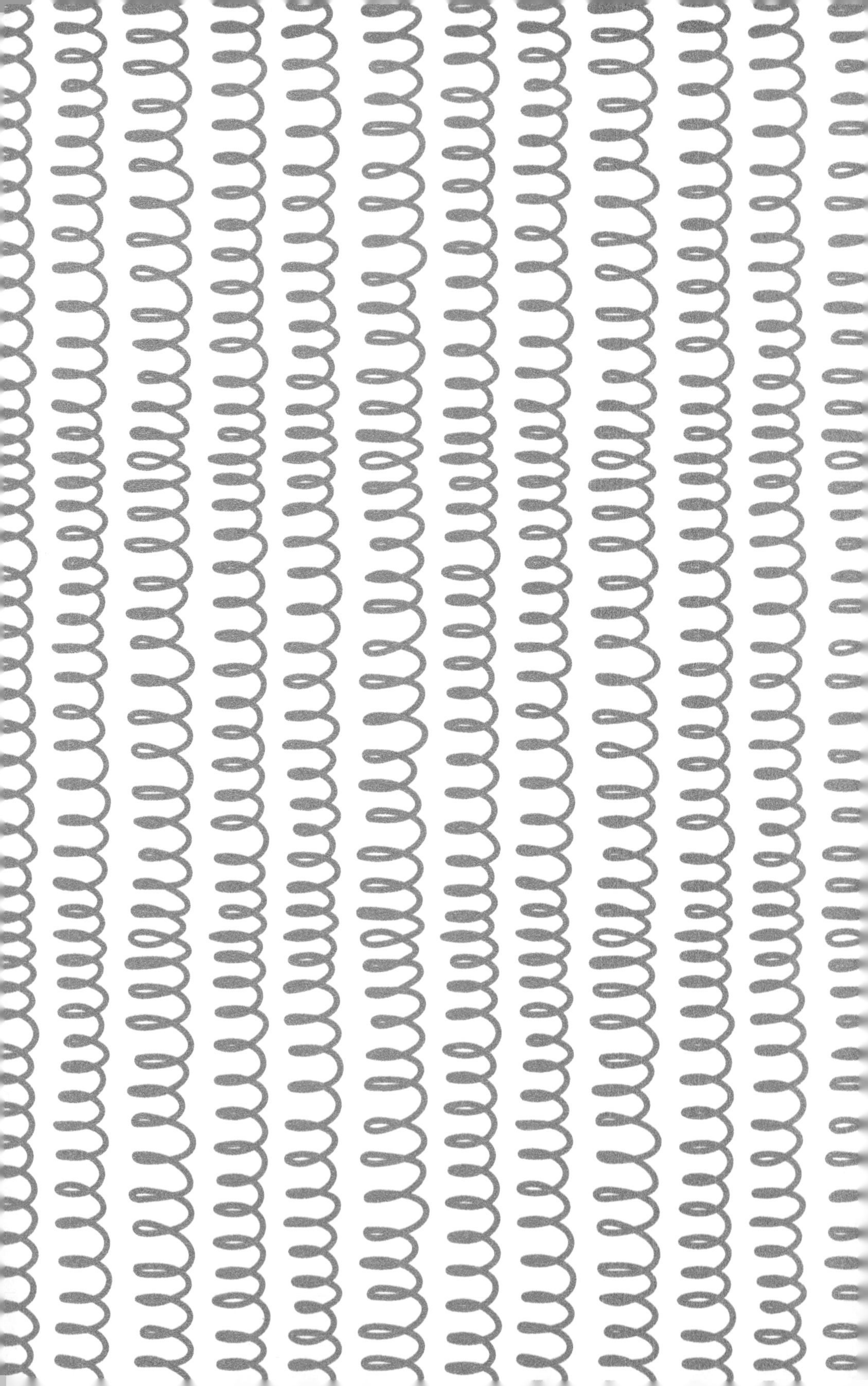

DESSERTS

Miss Wood sliced the small Twelfth Night cake into three pieces and laid each one on a nursery-sized plate. “Give the first to your father, dearest.”

Caroline walked carefully, slowly, around the table and laid the tiny plate in front of Layton. “Did I do good, Papa?” she whispered.

“’Twas perfect, love,” Layton answered in a matching whisper and kissed her on the forehead. She giggled and returned to the cake, pulling one plate in front of her own chair before sitting down, the picture of feminine demureness. Miss Wood had, apparently, been instructing Caroline in her mealtime manners.

“Can we look for the coin now?” Caroline asked Miss Wood, her eagerness belying her patient demeanor.

"That would be up to your father, Miss Caroline," Miss Wood answered gently. Miss Wood turned to look at Layton, expectation brightening her eyes. Something akin to mischief showed in the pair of chocolate-brown eyes. Brown. Why had he never noticed that before? It was an unusual combination: red hair and brown eyes. Yet it fit her somehow, surprisingly and unexpectedly.

"I think we'd better begin our search, Caroline. I'm anxious enough I just might eat the coin and not realize it."

"Oh, Papa!" Caroline giggled. "You are funny tonight!"

Drops of Gold
Sarah M Eden

Layton & Caroline's Twelfth Night Cake

Cake:
1¾ cups all-purpose flour
1½ teaspoons baking powder
¼ teaspoon baking soda
1 teaspoon salt
1 cup milk
¼ cup sour cream
1 tablespoon vinegar
¾ cup butter, at room temperature
1 cup sugar
2 teaspoons vanilla extract
3 large eggs, whites only

Buttercream frosting:
⅓ cup butter, room temperature
4½ cups powdered sugar, divided
¼ cup milk, plus more if needed
1½ teaspoons vanilla extract

For the cake:
Preheat oven to 350°F.

Line the bottom of three 6-inch round pans with parchment paper.

In a medium bowl, whisk together flour, baking powder, baking soda, and salt.

In a small bowl, whisk together milk, sour cream, and vinegar.

In a large bowl, cream the butter and sugar. Mix in vanilla extract. Beat in egg whites one at a time. Once the oven is fully preheated, add flour mixture to egg mixture. Mix until just combined. Add milk mixture and stir until combined. Pour into parchment-lined pans and place in the oven.

Bake for 30 minutes or until a toothpick inserted in the centers comes out clean. The top will not necessarily be golden. Remove pans from oven and allow cakes to cool completely. Turn out cakes from pans.

For the frosting:
Beat butter until fluffy. Add 2 cups powdered sugar. Beat well. Beat in milk and vanilla. Add in remaining powdered sugar until the frosting reaches a spreadable but not overly soft consistency. If frosting is too stiff, add in additional milk one teaspoon at a time until desired consistency is reached.

Frosting can grow overly soft when warm. If needed, place in refrigerator for a few minutes.

To assemble:
Using a knife, make a small slice in one cake, large enough for hiding a coin. This can be a party favor version or a real coin wrapped in foil for sanitary purposes or a bean wrapped in foil to make it easier to find.

Layer one cake on top of the other, with buttercream in between. Frost outside of stacked cakes with buttercream. Decorate, as desired, with white sprinkles, nonpareils, cake flowers, etc.

The person to find the coin or bean in their slice of cake on Twelfth Night is crowned monarch for the night and leads the evening's festivities.

Yields 6–8 servings.

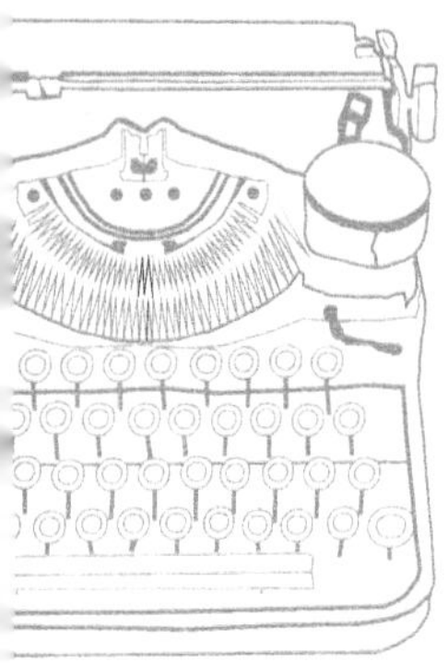

“These are very good,” Evan said, helping himself to another Welsh cake.

“Thank you,” Annie said, secretly pleased that he liked them. “It’s one of my mother’s recipes.”

“She must have been a good cook.”

Within the Dark Hills
Sian Ann Bessey

That is a very large frying pan, was the last lucid thought he had before everything around him went black.

As You Are
Sarah M. Eden

Welsh Cakes

2 cups flour
1 teaspoon baking powder
Pinch of salt
½ cup cold butter
½ cup sugar
½ cup raisins or sultanas
1 egg, lightly beaten
2–4 tablespoons milk

Sift the flour, baking powder, and salt together. Grate or cut the cold butter into small pieces. Rub butter into the flour mixture until it resembles breadcrumbs. Stir in the sugar and fruit. Add lightly beaten egg, then enough milk to form a dough.

Roll out dough to a thickness of ¼ inch, and cut into 3-inch circles.

Cook on a greased, hot griddle or thick frying pan for 2–3 minutes on each side or until the cakes are golden brown. Set on a wire rack to cool and sprinkle with sugar or serve warm with butter.

Yields approximately 30 Welsh cakes.

She dropped her gaze and shook her head.

"I need to know." He tried to coax her eyes upward by gently stroking her hair. The gesture didn't seem to impact her, though it had a most decided effect on himself. His heart raced, as it seemed to every time he touched her . . .

"You . . ." A jumpy breath cut off her words.

Crispin tensed. He had done something. If his unknown infraction had brought her to tears, he must have done something horrible. He'd find a way to make it up to her if he ever found out what he'd done.

"You ate the last fairy cake," Catherine whispered.

"I . . ." Her words were so unexpected Crispin could hardly digest them. "Fairy cake?"

"You didn't even save me one." Catherine gave him a look of complete disdain ruined by the twinkle of mischief in her still-wet eyes and the twitch he'd come to recognize as a smile fighting to be let free.

The Kiss of a Stranger
Sarah M. Eden

Fairy Cakes

Cakes:
½ cup butter, softened
½ cup superfine sugar
2 large eggs

1 teaspoon vanilla
¾ cup all-purpose flour
1½ teaspoons baking powder
1–2 tablespoons milk

Icing:
1 cup powdered sugar
1–2 tablespoons water
1 drop food coloring

For the cakes:
Preheat oven to 350°F.

Line a fairy cake tin or miniature cupcake tin with paper baking cups.

In a mixing bowl, cream butter and sugar. Beat in the eggs one at a time. Stir in the vanilla.

Combine flour and baking powder, then fold into the wet mixture. Add a little milk at a time until batter reaches a good dropping consistency. Spoon into the cup-lined tins until half full—don't overfill or the fairy cakes will collapse.

Bake for 8–10 minutes. Tops should be golden brown. Allow to cool for 10 minutes before removing from the tin. Cool cakes on a wire rack.

For the icing:
Sift powdered sugar into a mixing bowl. Stir in enough water to create a smooth mixture. Add a drop of food coloring. Drizzle icing over cooled cakes. Add sprinkles, nonpareils, sugar pearls, etc., if desired.

Serve once icing has hardened.

Yields approximately 36 miniature cupcakes.

One of my favorite ways to celebrate a new manuscript submission is to make this traditional English cake.

Sian Ann Bessey

Victoria Sandwich

Yellow Cake:
⅔ cup butter, softened
1¾ cups sugar
2 large eggs
1½ teaspoons vanilla extract
2½ cups flour
2½ teaspoons baking powder
½ teaspoon salt
1¼ cups milk

Buttercream frosting:
½ cup butter, softened
1½ teaspoons vanilla
2 cups powdered sugar
2–4 tablespoons cream or milk

Strawberry jam
Powdered sugar

For the cake:
Preheat oven to 350°F. Grease and line two 9-inch round baking pans with parchment paper.

In a large mixing bowl, cream butter and sugar until light and fluffy. Add eggs, one at a time, beating well after each addition. Stir in vanilla. In another bowl, combine the flour, baking powder, and salt. Add half the flour mixture to the creamed mixture then add the milk, followed by the remaining flour mixture. Beat well after each addition.

Divide batter equally between the two pans. Bake for 25–30 minutes or until a toothpick inserted near the center comes out clean. Cool for 10 minutes before removing from pans to wire racks to cool completely.

For the frosting:
Beat the butter until it is very smooth. Add vanilla, powdered sugar, and 2 tablespoons cream. Beat well. If necessary, add more cream until frosting reaches a good spreading consistency.

To assemble:
Set one of the cakes on a plate, upside down. Spread with a layer of strawberry jam. Top with the buttercream frosting and the second cake. Using a small sieve, dust the top of the cake with powdered sugar.

Note: Originally, a Victoria Sandwich was a simple yellow sponge cake with strawberry jam filling. Nowadays, a British bakery serves it with either strawberry jam and whipped cream in the center, or strawberry jam and buttercream frosting.

Yields 12 servings.

"Would you like to take some refreshment beneath the canopy now, my lady?" she asked Lady Langton.

"Very much," Lady Langton said with alacrity. "I wish you to try the orange-flower-water cake and tell me if you've ever tasted the like."

The Noble Smuggler
Sian Ann Bessey

Finley Park's Orange Blossom Cake

Cake:
2 cups flour
½ cup cornstarch
2 teaspoons baking powder
½ teaspoon salt
2 cups sugar
1 cup olive oil
Zest from one orange and one lemon
5 large eggs
Juice from one orange and one lemon plus enough sour cream or plain yogurt to equal 1 cup

Glaze:
¼ cup orange juice
¼ cup sugar
½ teaspoon orange blossom extract

White chocolate ganache:
¼ cup white chocolate chips
¼ cup cream

For the cake:
Grease a bundt pan. Preheat oven to 350°F.

In a medium-sized bowl, mix flour, cornstarch, baking powder, and salt. Set aside.

Using the whisk attachment in the bowl of a stand mixer, beat the sugar, oil, and zest on high speed until blended. Add eggs, one at a time, beating well after each addition. Continue beating until the mixture is thick and pale.

In a liquid measuring cup, combine the juice of one orange, one lemon, plus enough sour cream or plain yogurt to equal 1 cup. Add half this mixture to the sugar and eggs, followed by half the flour mixture. Beat until just blended. Add remaining juice mixture, followed by the remaining flour mixture. Mix well and pour into the bundt pan.

Bake for 50–60 minutes or until a toothpick inserted into the middle comes out clean. Cool the cake in the pan for 5–10 minutes before inverting onto a cooling rack.

For the glaze:
While the cake is cooling, mix the orange juice and sugar in a small saucepan. Heat until the sugar is dissolved. Take off the heat and add orange blossom extract. Using a pastry brush, spread the liquid over the warm cake to seal in the moisture.

For the ganache:
Put white chocolate chips and cream in a microwave-safe bowl and heat for 30 seconds. Stir. If the chocolate chips have not dissolved, heat a little longer. When the chocolate chips and cream are well blended, put the bowl in the fridge to cool. Stir every 10 minutes, until the ganache has thickened. Drizzle over the cooled cake.

Yields 12 servings.

"Did I mention that I made cheesecake for dessert?"

Taylor laughed now. "Boy, did I pick the right day to show up at your house."

Smoke Screen
Traci Hunter Abramson

Cheesecake

Crust*:
1¼ cups graham cracker crumbs (1 sleeve)
4 tablespoons butter, softened

Cheesecake:
3 (8-ounce) packages of cream cheese, softened
3 eggs
1 cup sugar
2 teaspoons vanilla

Preheat oven to 350°F.

For the crust:
Blend graham cracker crumbs with softened butter and press into the bottom of a 9-inch springform pan. Set aside.

For the cheesecake:
Beat softened cream cheese until no lumps remain. Add eggs, sugar, and vanilla. Beat until smooth. Pour over crust.

Bake 40 minutes. Place directly into the refrigerator to stop the cooking action. Chill in the refrigerator for at least two hours.

If desired, serve with fresh fruit, chocolate syrup, or fruit syrup.

*Alternative gluten-free crust:
1½ cups almond flour
¼ cup brown sugar
4 tablespoons butter, melted

Combine all three ingredients and press into the bottom of a 9-inch springform pan. Bake at 350°F for 8 minutes. Cool completely before filling with cheesecake mixture.

Yields 8–12 servings.

"I would say that we could have some leftover cheesecake." Riley looked pointedly at Tristan.

He gave her a sheepish grin. "Yeah, well, the guys said to thank you for that."

"What guys?" Taylor looked from Riley to Tristan. "What did happen to the cheesecake? I was looking for that earlier."

Riley shifted her attention to Taylor. "My darling husband decided he wanted some for breakfast and then had the brilliant idea that the other guys in the squad would probably like some too."

"For breakfast?"

Smoke Screen
Traci Hunter Abramson

Chocolate Cheesecake

Crust*:
1¼ cups crushed graham crackers (1 sleeve)
4 tablespoons butter, melted

Cheesecake:
½ cup sugar
11 ounces cream cheese, softened
½ cup butter, softened
7 ounces semi-sweet chocolate chips
10 ounces whipping cream

For the crust:
Mix graham crackers and melted butter and press into the bottom of a 9-inch springform pan.

For the cheesecake:
Cream together sugar, cream cheese, and butter until smooth. Melt chocolate chips in microwave or over a double boiler and add to the cream cheese mixture. Stir until well blended.

In a separate bowl, whip cream until thick. Fold gently into the chocolate mixture. Pour over the graham cracker base and smooth the surface with the back of a spoon. Chill for two hours, or until firm.

*Alternative gluten-free crust:
1½ cups almond flour
¼ cup brown sugar
4 tablespoons butter, melted

Combine all three ingredients and press into the bottom of a 9-inch springform pan. Bake at 350°F for 8 minutes. Cool completely before filling with cheesecake mixture.

Yields 8–12 servings.

On the first Thanksgiving he'd spent with them, Steve had tasted Dorcas's homemade apple pie, and he hadn't left the table until he'd finished the entire dish. From that time on, he had requested Dorcas's apple pie for birthdays and Christmases, along with the next three Thanksgivings.

The Gem Thief
Sian Ann Bessey

Dorcas's Apple Pie

Pastry*:
2½ cups flour
1 teaspoon salt
1 cup shortening
1 egg, beaten
1 tablespoon vinegar
¼ cup cold water

(This makes enough pastry for two double-crust pies or four pie shells. If making only one pie, divide the dough in two and refrigerate or freeze one portion for later use, as directed in the recipe.)

Filling:
6–7 Granny Smith apples, peeled, cored, and thinly sliced
½ tablespoon lemon juice
½ teaspoon cinnamon

¼ teaspoon salt
½ cup sugar
3 tablespoons cornstarch
1 egg, beaten

For the pastry:
In a large bowl, mix dry ingredients. Cut in shortening with a pastry cutter or two knives or rub in with fingers until mixture resembles crumbs. Form a well in the center. Fill with beaten egg, vinegar, and water. Blend with a fork until the mixture comes together to form a dough. Divide in two. Wrap both pieces in plastic wrap. Freeze one portion for future use and chill the other in the fridge while preparing the filling.

For the filling:
Place apple slices in a large bowl and gently toss with lemon juice, cinnamon, salt, sugar, and cornstarch.

Preheat oven to 425°F.

Divide chilled dough into two. Roll out first portion into a 12-inch circle and transfer to a 9-inch pie pan. Trim edges. Add apple mixture, mounding slightly in the center. Roll second crust into an 11-inch circle. Carefully set it on top of the apples. Seal and crimp edges.

Using a sharp knife, cut half a dozen small slits in pastry top to allow steam to escape. Brush with beaten egg.

Bake for 15 minutes. Lower the oven temperature to 350°F and cook an additional 40–50 minutes.

*To make this pie gluten-free, use the GF pastry recipe on pages 252–253.

Yields 8 servings.

A hint of a smile crept onto Elise's face. "We picnicked under our tree quite often."

"Do you remember the one when you refused to eat anything that wasn't red?" The Epsworth cook had actually enjoyed trying to put together an entirely red picnic. Everyone had adored Elise.

"I don't believe I've ever eaten so many strawberries in a single meal."

For Elise
Sarah M. Eden

Strawberry Pie

1 cup cold water
3 tablespoons cornstarch
½ cup sugar
1 (3-ounce) box strawberry Jell-O
1 pint fresh strawberries, tops removed, sliced in half lengthwise
1 (9-inch) pie crust (baked or graham cracker)

Mix water, cornstarch, and sugar in a small saucepan. Bring to boil over medium heat and cook until thickened. Add Jell-O and stir well.

Place berries in pie crust, then pour Jell-O mixture over berries. Chill for several hours. Serve with whipped cream.

Yields 8 servings.

"There are mince pies?" Giles's excitement knew no bounds.

"I've never known Cook to miss a year," Philip said.

Giles waded through the snow to reclaim his sledge. "Mince pies, Mia! We must hurry."

A Season of Hope
Sian Ann Bessey

Traditional English Mince Pies

Pastry:
2½ cups flour
1 teaspoon salt
1 cup shortening
1 egg, beaten
1 tablespoon vinegar
¼ cup cold water

Filling:
2 (411-gram [approximately 14-ounce]) jar of mincemeat (Robertson's brand, imported from the UK, is the best)
1 apple, peeled and grated

Sugar for sprinkling

Preheat oven to 400°F.

For the pastry:
In a large bowl, mix dry ingredients. Cut in shortening with a pastry cutter or two knives or rub in with fingers until mixture resembles crumbs. Form a well in the center. Fill with beaten egg, vinegar, and water. Blend with a fork until the mixture comes together to form a dough. Wrap dough in plastic wrap and chill while preparing the filling.

For the filling:
In a bowl, mix mincemeat and grated apple.

Roll pastry into a large sheet, approximately ⅛-inch thick. With a round pastry cutter, cut out twenty-four 3½-inch disks of pastry. Press circles into the bottom of two 12-count muffin pans and fill each pastry base with 1 tablespoon of the mincemeat mixture.

With a 2½-inch round cutter, cut 24 pastry circles for the lids. If necessary, gather the pastry scraps into a ball and roll out again to create enough pastry circles. Place pastry lid on top of each miniature pie, gently pushing down around the edges to seal. Sprinkle with sugar.

Bake for 15–20 minutes and then transfer to a wire rack to cool. Serve warm with cream or cold with powdered sugar dusted on the top.

Yields 24 miniature pies.

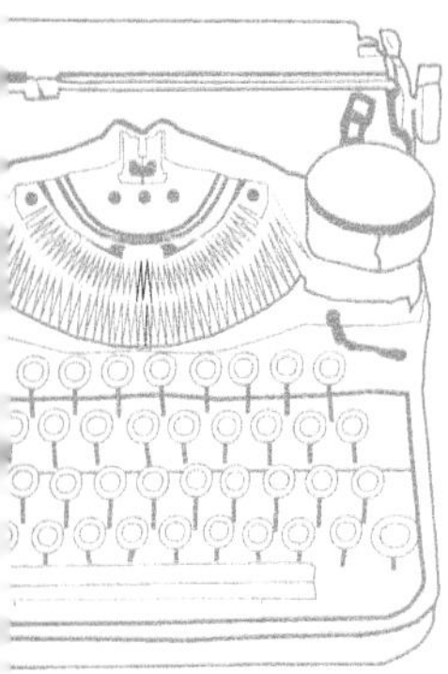

James discovered that doing a kindness for Daphne was both a privilege and a joy. He'd spent an enjoyable afternoon and morning planning the impromptu picnic. By means of a quick *tête-à-tête* with Her Grace at the Bowers' musicale the evening before, he'd discovered Daphne liked water-chestnut sandwiches, lemonade, and apple tarts. He'd also learned that the Lancasters had enjoyed only the most basic of accommodations when picnicking: a blanket, a basket of food, plates, and utensils. He meant to recreate those excursions.

Romancing Daphne
Sarah M. Eden

"You must bring your berry tart again, Katie," Mrs. O'Connor said. "No one bakes a tart as well as you do."

Love Remains
Sarah M. Eden

Two cups of coffee, a slice of berry tart, a cheese-and-prosciutto-filled crusty roll, and three croissants later, Quinn thought he might live to see another day after all.

The Gem Thief
Sian Ann Bessey

Fruit Tart

Pastry:
1½ cups all-purpose flour
1 tablespoon sugar
½ teaspoon salt
1 teaspoon freshly grated lemon zest
10 tablespoons cold butter, cut into small pieces
4 tablespoons very cold water

Filling:
½ cup sugar
¼ cup cornstarch
3 cups mixed berries, divided
1 teaspoon freshly grated lemon zest

For the pastry:
Pulse flour, sugar, and salt in a food processor to mix well. Add lemon zest and butter. Pulse until the mixture takes on a sandy texture. With the processor running, slowly add water until moist clumps form. Mixture should barely hold together when pressed.

Turn onto a lightly floured surface and form into a ball. Place in the center of a large piece of plastic wrap. Press dough down into a disk, no more than 2 inches thick. Wrap in plastic wrap, pressing together any breaks in the edges of the dough.

Refrigerate for at least an hour.

For the tarts:
Preheat oven to 400°F.

Let dough rest outside of the refrigerator until room temperature. Roll out on a lightly floured surface into a 11–12-inch circle. Carefully transfer to a 9-inch tart pan. Press carefully into the fluted edge. Roll the rolling pin over the rim to trim off excess dough. Neaten the edge if needed. Prick the bottom of the pastry with a fork several times.

Place in the freezer for 10 minutes. (Skip this step if using a Pyrex or glass pan, as sudden changes in temperature increase the risk of these pans shattering.)

Line the dough with parchment paper and add pie weights or dried beans. Blind-bake pastry for 25 minutes or until the crust begins to darken.

Reduce oven temperature to 350°F and remove the tart shell. Remove the parchment and weights/beans.

For the filling:
In a medium mixing bowl, mix sugar and cornstarch. Add 2 cups of berries and the lemon zest. Mash enough for some of the berries to dissolve into the sugar mixture. Pour into the tart shell. Top with remaining berries.

Place on a baking sheet and bake for 30–40 minutes, until the filling starts to bubble (the simmering is what sets the filling). If the shell starts to brown too deeply, cover it loosely with foil.

Allow to cool entirely before serving. Particularly good served with whipped cream, vanilla ice cream, or crème fraiche.

Yields 8 servings.

"You're welcome." Reed smiled. "Of course, if you really want to show me how grateful you are, you'll make that cherry cobbler for dessert tomorrow night."

"Why not tonight?"

"I didn't want to press my luck," Reed said. "You've had a pretty full day."

"That's an understatement."

Tripwire
Traci Hunter Abramson

Cherry Cobbler

Crumble topping:
¾ cup flour
⅓ cup brown sugar
⅓ cup sugar
1 teaspoon cinnamon
½ cup cold butter

Cobbler base:
¼ cup butter, melted
1 cup flour
¾ cup sugar
¼ cup brown sugar
1 cup milk
1 (21-ounce) can cherry pie filling

Preheat oven to 350°F.

For the crumble topping:
In a large bowl mix flour, brown sugar, sugar, and cinnamon. Cut butter into dry ingredients. Use a fork to mix until the dry ingredients resemble large crumbs. Set aside.

For the cobbler base:
Spread melted butter in bottom of a 9 x 13-inch pan. In a large bowl, combine flour, sugar, brown sugar, and milk. Pour into pan. Do not stir with butter. Spoon cherry pie filling over batter. Do not stir. Sprinkle crumble topping evenly over the top of the cherry filling. Bake for 35 minutes.

If desired, serve with ice cream.

Yields 10–12 servings.

"You can make baklava?" Noah stared at her for a brief moment and then wrapped his arms around her waist. "Marry me."

For a split second, Kelsey wondered if he might be serious. Then she saw the corner of his lips twitch up into a half smile. With a shake of her head, she said, "Vegas isn't currently in my plans."

Deep Cover
Traci Hunter Abramson

"I hope you saved room for dessert."

"Baklava?" The single word escaped JD in a reverent whisper.

"Baklava," Kelsey confirmed.

Mistaken Reality
Traci Hunter Abramson

Baklava

Syrup:
1 cup sugar
¼ teaspoon cinnamon
½ cup honey
1½ tablespoons lemon juice
¾ cup water

Filling:
3½ cup walnuts, coarsely ground
1 cup pistachios, coarsely ground
2 tablespoons sugar
1 teaspoon cinnamon
¼ teaspoon cloves

Dough:
16-ounce package frozen phyllo dough
½ cup melted butter

Preheat oven to 325°F.

Thaw phyllo dough according to package directions.

For the syrup:
In a small saucepan, combine sugar, cinnamon, honey, lemon juice, and water. Boil over medium-high heat until sugar dissolves. Reduce heat to medium-low. Boil an additional 4 minutes without stirring. Remove from heat and set aside.

For the filling:
Stir together filling ingredients in a bowl. Set aside.

To assemble:
Lightly brush butter on a sheet of phyllo dough and place sheet in a greased 9 x 13-inch pan. Repeat 10 times, layering a total of 10 sheets of buttered phyllo dough as the base. Sprinkle ⅕ of the nut mixture on top of the phyllo dough. Layer 5 more sheets of buttered phyllo dough on top of the nut mixture and sprinkle ⅕ of the nut mixture on top. Repeat process three more times. Top with the last fifth of the nut mixture. Top with 10 more buttered phyllo sheets.

Cut pastry into 1½-inch-wide strips. Then cut diagonally to form diamond shapes. Bake for 35 minutes or until the top is golden brown.

Remove from oven and immediately spoon the cooled syrup evenly over the hot baklava. (Note: It isn't necessary to use all of the syrup. For a less sticky version, use approximately half.) Let baklava cool completely, uncovered, at room temperature. For best results, let sit for at least 4 hours before serving.

Yields 32 pieces.

"Do you suppose we'll have bread pudding again today?" Oliver asked, his voice quiet and sleepy.

"As this is Artemis's house, I cannot imagine we will not," His Grace said.

"Bread pudding is her most favorite."

Charming Artemis
Sarah M. Eden

Alexander grinned. He and Cook had a long history that had begun with him pilfering bread pudding from the kitchen when he was a boy and had developed into her making it especially for him whenever he returned home.

"If Cook happens to have any extra bread pudding in the kitchen, I would be happy to take it off her hands," he said.

An Uncommon Earl
Sian Ann Bessey

Bread Pudding

6 slices of slightly stale cinnamon raisin bread
2 tablespoons melted butter
4 large eggs
2 cups milk
¾ cup sugar
1 teaspoon vanilla extract

Preheat oven to 350°F.

Break cinnamon bread into small pieces. Drop into an 8-inch square baking pan and spread out evenly. Drizzle melted butter over the bread.

In a mixing bowl, beat eggs, milk, sugar, and vanilla. Pour over bread. Lightly push down the bread to make certain it is covered and soaking up the egg & milk mixture.

Bake for 45 minutes. Top will be springy.

Yields 8–10 servings.

Before long, they reached the vacant table and took their seats. Instantly, a servant appeared at Lady Langton's side to offer her tea and her choice of divine-looking cakes and pastries.

The Noble Smuggler
Sian Ann Bessey

Finley Park Cream Puffs

Pastry dough:
1 cup water
½ cup butter
1 cup flour*
Pinch of salt
4 large eggs

Custard filling:
2 cups milk
½ cup sugar
3 tablespoons cornstarch
1 egg
2 tablespoons butter
1 teaspoon vanilla extract
½ teaspoon almond extract

Whipped cream filling:
1 cup whipping cream
1 tablespoon powdered sugar

Chocolate ganache:
⅔ cup semi-sweet chocolate chips
⅔ cup heavy cream

Preheat oven to 400°F. Line baking sheets with parchment paper and set aside.

For the pastry:
In a medium saucepan, bring water and butter to a boil. Add flour and salt and stir with a wooden spoon until fully incorporated and the mixture looks like Play-Doh.

Place hot dough into the mixing bowl of a stand mixer fitted with a paddle attachment. Beat on medium speed to cool dough. Add eggs one at a time, beating well after each addition. Beat until dough is smooth.

Spoon dough onto baking sheets to form circles approximately 1½ inches across. Maintain a 1½–2-inch space between spoonfuls to allow for rising. Bake for 30 minutes. Turn off the oven, open the door, and pierce each cream puff with a sharp knife. This will help the steam inside to escape and the cream puff to crisp up. Leave the cream puffs in the oven with the door open a few inches until the oven has cooled completely.

For the custard:
In a saucepan, mix milk, sugar, cornstarch, and egg. Heat and stir with a whisk until mixture comes to a boil. Cook for 1 minute.

Take off the heat. Add butter and extracts. Stir until well blended.

Pour into a bowl. Cover with a piece of plastic wrap, gently pressing the wrap until it touches the custard. This will prevent a skin from forming as the custard cools. Place in refrigerator until cool.

For the whipped cream:
Using a chilled bowl and beaters, whip cream until soft peaks form. Add powdered sugar. Whip until blended.

To assemble:
Slice open the cream puffs. Fill the center with a spoonful of custard and a spoonful of whipped cream, and then replace the top.

For the ganache:
Place chocolate chips and cream in a microwave-safe bowl. Heat for 1 minute. Remove from microwave and stir well. If needed, heat an additional 30 seconds and stir again. Repeat until the chocolate and cream are well mixed. Place in refrigerator and allow to cool, stirring every 10 minutes. When chocolate has thickened but is still pourable, drizzle over the cream puffs.

Alternatively, omit ganache topping and dust cream puffs with powdered sugar.

*To make the cream puffs gluten-free, substitute flour with:
⅔ cup white rice flour
⅓ cup sweet rice flour
½ teaspoon xanthan gum
1 teaspoon baking powder

Mix these ingredients together and add as one to the water, salt, and butter in the saucepan. Continue as directed in the recipe.

Yields 18–24 cream puffs.

Patrick spotted, at the very end of the table, his ma's shortbread. She'd always cut it in triangles and sprinkled sugar on top. She'd now and then added cardamom when it was available, on account of Grady preferring it that way. No matter how she made shortbread, Patrick loved it. To him, it was the taste of home.

Valley of Dreams
Sarah M. Eden

Cardamom Shortbread

1⅔ cups all-purpose flour
1 tablespoon cornstarch
½ + ⅛ teaspoon ground cardamom
½ teaspoon table salt
¾ cup butter, unsalted

⅔ cup powdered sugar
½ teaspoon vanilla extract
Extra butter for the pan

Preheat oven to 325°F.

Whisk the flour, cornstarch, cardamom, and salt in a medium bowl.

In a large bowl, beat butter, powdered sugar, and vanilla until creamy. Add the flour mixture a little at a time, mixing on low speed, until the dough reaches a crumbly texture.

Lightly butter the bottom of an 8 x 8-inch pan.

Pour crumbly dough into the buttered pan. With lightly floured fingers, press the dough into the pan to spread evenly and press into a firm solid. With a thin, sharp knife, lightly floured, cut the dough all the way through into 18 rectangular bars or 9 wider bars cut diagonally into triangles. With a lightly floured fork, prick each bar or triangle, evenly spaced, twice all the way through.

Place the pan in the freezer until the oven finishes heating. (Skip this step if using a Pyrex or glass pan, as sudden changes in temperature increase the risk of these pans shattering.)

Bake on the center rack for 35–40 minutes, turning the pan at the halfway point. The top will turn golden brown and look quite dry. Remove from the oven and place the pan on a wire cooling rack. Using the knife, re-cut the cookies. Once the shortbread is completely cooled, remove from the pan.

Yields 18 cookies.

The smell of roasted almonds and gingerbread wafted on the air, making Lars wish he'd arrived early enough to sample them before his appointment at the bank.

The Danger with Diamonds
Traci Hunter Abramson and Sian Ann Bessey

Christmas Market Gingerbread Men

10 tablespoons butter, softened
¾ cup brown sugar
⅔ cup molasses
1 egg
1 teaspoon vanilla
3½ cups flour
1 teaspoon baking soda
½ teaspoon salt
3 teaspoons ground ginger
3 teaspoons cinnamon
½ teaspoon allspice
½ teaspoon ground cloves

In a stand mixer, beat butter until smooth and creamy. Add brown sugar and molasses and beat until well combined. Add egg and vanilla. Beat on high speed for 2 minutes. On low speed, add flour, baking soda, salt, ginger, cinnamon, allspice, and cloves. The dough will be heavy and a little sticky.

Divide dough in half and shape into disks. Wrap each disk in plastic wrap and chill for a couple of hours or overnight. Do not skip this step.

Preheat oven to 350°F.

Line 2–3 baking sheets with parchment paper. Remove chilled dough from fridge. It will be quite hard. If necessary, allow the dough to soften slightly on the counter before rolling out on a floured surface until the dough is about ¼-inch thick. Cut into shapes of choice and place about an inch apart on the baking sheets. Re-roll scraps and repeat.

Bake for 8–10 minutes. Allow cookies to cool on the pan for 5 minutes before transferring to a cooling rack. Once completely cooled, decorate as desired.

Yields 24–30 cookies (depending on size of cutout).

She pointed to the basket Emily held. “There’s some of the baron’s favorite biscuits in that one. Make sure he knows.”

An Alleged Rogue
Sian Ann Bessey

Lord Dunsbourne’s Oatmeal Biscuits

1 cup butter, softened
⅔ cup light brown sugar
⅓ cup sugar
1 teaspoon vanilla
2 large eggs
1½ cups flour
½ teaspoon cinnamon
½ teaspoon baking soda
½ teaspoon baking powder
½ teaspoon salt
2½ cups old-fashioned rolled oats
1 cup raisins

*For a modern addition, add 1 cup chopped pecans and/or 1 cup chocolate chips.

Preheat oven to 350°F. Line a baking sheet with parchment paper.

Beat softened butter and sugars together until smooth. Add vanilla and eggs, one egg at a time. Add flour, cinnamon, baking soda, baking powder, and salt. Mix until combined. Add oats, followed by raisins (and nuts or chocolate chips, if desired).

Scoop dough into 1½-inch balls and place on baking sheet about two inches apart. Bake 8–12 minutes (until golden brown on edges but with the center still looking slightly under-baked). Allow to cool for 5 minutes on the baking sheet and then transfer to a cooling rack.

Yields approximately 40 biscuits/cookies.

Tip: The longer the dough sits on the counter before baking, the thicker the cookies will be because the oatmeal will absorb some of the moisture.

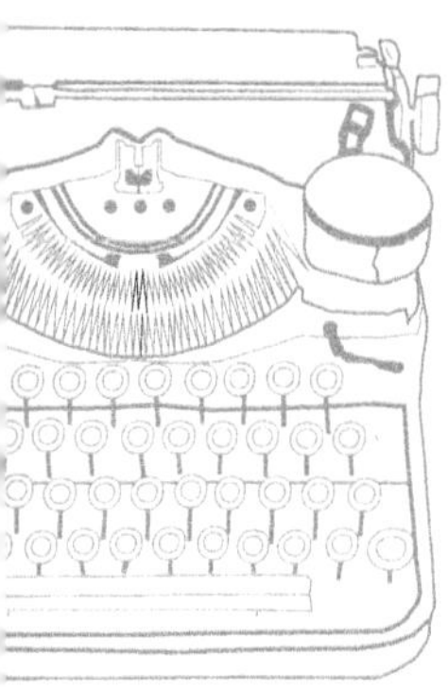

[Jason] tied his stem of grass into interlocking circles, just as Mater had always done when the two of them had sat on the banks of the Trent eating pilfered ginger biscuits and talking at length on any number of subjects.

A Fine Gentleman
Sarah M. Eden

Mater's Ginger Biscuits

2¼ cups all-purpose flour
1 teaspoon baking soda
¾ teaspoon ground cinnamon
½ teaspoon ground cloves
2 teaspoons ground ginger
¼ teaspoon salt
¾ cup butter, softened
1 cup sugar
1 large egg
¼ cup brown sugar
2 tablespoons water
2 tablespoons superfine sugar (can substitute with white sugar)

Preheat oven to 350°F.

In a medium bowl, mix flour, baking soda, cinnamon, cloves, ginger, and salt.

In a large bowl, cream butter and white sugar. Beat in the egg. Beat in the brown sugar and water. Gradually stir the dry ingredients from the medium bowl into the large bowl until all ingredients are well mixed.

Spread superfine sugar on a shallow plate. Shape dough into balls and roll them in the sugar. Place the cookies on an ungreased baking sheet and flatten slightly.

Bake for 8–10 minutes. Do not overbake. Cookies will stiffen as they cool, and overbaked cookies will get hard.

Yields approximately 2 dozen cookies.

There were globs of frosting all over the counter, smears of food coloring on her fingers, and almost every bowl, knife, and spoon she owned was dirty. It was a total disaster, but as she studied the pan of sugar cookies sitting in the middle of the chaos, she couldn't help but smile. Walter would love them.

The Gem Thief
Sian Ann Bessey

Sugar Cookies

Cookies:
½ cup butter
1 cup sugar
2 large eggs
½ cup plain yogurt or sour cream
1 teaspoon vanilla
3½ cups flour
1 teaspoon baking powder
½ teaspoon baking soda
½ teaspoon salt

Frosting:
½ cup butter, softened
2½ cups powdered sugar, divided
3 tablespoons heavy cream
1 teaspoon vanilla
Food coloring of choice (optional)

Preheat oven to 350°F.

For the cookies:
Cream the butter. Add sugar until well blended. Add eggs, yogurt or sour cream, and vanilla. Mix well. Add dry ingredients and mix until a thick dough forms.

Wrap dough in plastic wrap and chill in the refrigerator for 1 hour. Remove dough from wrapping and roll out on a lightly floured surface to a little over ¼-inch thick. Cut to desired shapes with cookie cutters and place 1 inch apart on baking sheets covered in parchment paper. Bake for 8–10 minutes. Remove from pans and place on a cooling rack.

For the frosting:
Beat butter until creamy. Add 1¼ cups of the powdered sugar. Mix. Add cream and vanilla. Mix. Add remaining powdered sugar. Beat for 1 minute. If the consistency is too thick, add another tablespoon of cream. Add food coloring, if desired.

Frost the cookies when they are completely cool.

Yields 24–36 cookies (depending on size of cookie cutters).

Tip: Do not cut the time short when mixing the frosting. The trick to creamy frosting is to beat it long enough that it is light and fluffy.

"Can I bring you back anything?"

"One of Miss Carol's chocolate chip cookies would be nice." He lowered his voice before adding, "The missus keeps trying to force that whole-grain nonsense on me."

"Just make sure you don't reveal your source."

"Deal."

Sanctuary
Traci Hunter Abramson

Miss Carol's Chocolate Chip Cookies

2¼ cups all-purpose flour
1 teaspoon baking soda
1½ teaspoons cinnamon
½ teaspoon salt
1 cup butter or margarine, softened
¾ cup sugar
¾ cup packed brown sugar
1 egg
1½ teaspoons vanilla
1 tablespoon milk
1 (12-ounce) package semi-sweet chocolate chips (2 cups)

Preheat oven to 375°F.

In a small bowl, combine flour, baking soda, cinnamon, and salt.

In a large bowl, cream together margarine, sugar, and brown sugar until well blended. Add the egg, vanilla, and milk. Mix well. Stir in flour mixture. When blended thoroughly, add chocolate chips.

Form into teaspoon-sized balls and place on ungreased baking sheet. Bake for 7–9 minutes.

Yields 4–5 dozen cookies.

Joe reached out, grabbed Katy's wrist, and took the knife. "Can I lick it?" he asked, just to torture her even more.

Rob roared with laughter, and Katy, valiantly trying to keep a straight face, snatched the knife back and said, "No, and if you don't start behaving better, you're not having any brownies either!"

Cover of Darkness
Sian Ann Bessey

Katy's Brownies

Brownies:
1 cup butter, melted
6 tablespoons cocoa powder
2 cups sugar
4 large eggs
2 cups flour
1 teaspoon vanilla
Dash of salt

Frosting:
½ cup butter, softened
2 cups powdered sugar
¼ cup cocoa powder
1 teaspoon vanilla
3–4 tablespoons heavy cream

Preheat oven to 350°F.

For the brownies:
In a small bowl, mix butter and cocoa powder until smooth and set aside.

In a large bowl, beat sugar and eggs until pale yellow and frothy. Add butter and cocoa mixture and mix well. Add flour, vanilla, and salt. Stir until just combined. Pour into a greased 9 x 13-inch pan and spread evenly. Bake for 25–30 minutes.

For the frosting:
Whip butter until creamy. Add powdered sugar, cocoa powder, vanilla, and 3 tablespoons cream. Mix gently, increasing speed as the ingredients are incorporated. Add more cream if necessary. Whip until fluffy. Spread on cooled brownie.

Yields 12–20 brownies.

"Can I ask why you're hiding mint brownies when you can just pick one up and eat it?"

"Oh, I already had one," Vanessa said mischievously. "I just want to make sure I can have another."

"There are at least three dozen brownies here."

"Yeah, but you don't know Quinn very well. He can eat a dozen by himself."

Drop Zone
Traci Hunter Abramson

Mint Brownies

Brownies:
¾ cup cocoa powder
2 cups sugar
1 cup butter or margarine, melted
1 teaspoon vanilla
4 large eggs
½ teaspoon salt
1½ cups flour

Mint icing:
½ cup butter, softened
2½ cups powdered sugar
2 tablespoons water
½ teaspoon peppermint extract
Green food coloring (optional)

Chocolate topping:
6 tablespoons butter
1 cup semi-sweet chocolate chips

Preheat oven to 325°F.

For the brownies:
Combine cocoa powder, sugar, and melted butter or margarine in a medium bowl. Add vanilla and eggs. Mix well. Add salt and flour. Stir until thoroughly combined. Spread batter in a 9 x 13-inch pan. Bake for 22–26 minutes or until a toothpick inserted an inch from the side comes out clean. Cool completely.

For the mint icing:
Combine ½ cup softened butter with powdered sugar, ½ cup at a time. Halfway through adding the powdered sugar, add water and peppermint extract, then continue adding powdered sugar ½ cup at a time until combined. If desired, add 2–3 drops of green food coloring. Spread icing onto cooled brownies. Refrigerate until firm, at least one hour.

For the chocolate topping:
Place 6 tablespoons butter and chocolate chips in a microwave-safe bowl. Microwave for one minute. Stir until smooth. Spread over mint icing. Refrigerate brownies for 1 hour before serving.

Yields 12–20 brownies.

“What would you like to have for dinner?”

Zoe looked thoughtful for a moment. “How ‘bout donuts?”

Ben couldn’t help it. He laughed.

The Insider
Sian Ann Bessey

Good-Enough-to-Have-for-Dinner Donuts

2 tablespoons yeast
1½ cups warm milk
1 cup cold mashed potatoes*
½ cup sugar
½ cup vegetable oil
2 teaspoons salt
2 teaspoons vanilla
½ teaspoon baking soda
½ teaspoon baking powder
2 large eggs
5½–6 cups flour
Vegetable or canola oil for frying

Glaze:
1½ cups powdered sugar
3–5 tablespoons water

For the donuts:
In a large mixing bowl, dissolve yeast in warm milk. Add potatoes, sugar, oil, salt, vanilla, baking soda, baking powder, and eggs. Mix well. Add enough flour to form a soft dough. Do not knead.

Place dough in a greased bowl, turning once to grease top. Cover and let rise in a warm place until doubled, about 1 hour.

Punch dough down. On a floured surface, roll dough out about ½-inch thick. Cut with a 3-inch donut cutter. Place donuts on greased baking sheets, cover, and let rise until almost doubled, about 45 minutes.

Heat 4–6 inches of oil to 350°F. Fry donuts until the lower side is golden brown. Flip and repeat on the other side. Remove donuts from oil and drain on paper towels. Roll in sugar, cinnamon-sugar, sugar glaze, or allow to cool and frost with your favorite frosting.

For the glaze:
Measure powdered sugar into a bowl. Add water 1 tablespoon at a time, mixing well between each addition until glaze reaches a thick but pourable consistency.

Yields about 3 dozen donuts.

*Tip: Use leftover mashed potatoes from an earlier meal or make up a small batch of mashed potatoes from dehydrated flakes.

"What was your father's favorite sweet?" she asked him.

"He never left a sweetshop without—"

"Peppermints," the older Jonquil brothers and Mater answered in unison.

Charming Artemis
Sarah M. Eden

Lucas's Peppermint Ice Cream

1½ cups whole milk
1½ cups half-and-half
2 cups heavy cream
1½ cups granulated sugar
¼ teaspoon salt
1 tablespoon vanilla extract
1 tablespoon peppermint extract
1 cup crushed peppermint candy (e.g., candy canes, peppermint sticks, Starlight mints, etc.)

Combine milk, half-and-half, and cream. Beat well with a hand mixer. Add sugar, salt, vanilla extract, and peppermint extract. Mix well to fully incorporate. Add in crushed peppermint candy. Stir well.

Pour mixture into an ice cream maker (recipe makes 2 quarts, so make certain your ice cream maker has a 2-quart capacity, or cut recipe in half). Follow manufacturer's directions for the ice cream maker.

Yields 2 quarts.

"Hey, what are friends for?" He smiled—a slightly crooked, wonderfully familiar smile. "Well, other than cheering you on in the 100 meters or swimming together in the canals or arguing over which is the best crepe at Crepe Affaire."

"Strawberries and cream," Tess said.

He chuckled. "Nutella. No question."

Heirs of Falcon Point
Traci Hunter Abramson, Sian Ann Bessey, Paige Edwards, and A. L. Sowards

Dessert Crepes

Crepe batter:
3 large eggs
1 cup milk
3 tablespoons butter, melted
1 cup flour*
½ teaspoon salt

Filling:
4 ounces cream cheese, softened
½ cup powdered sugar
½ teaspoon vanilla
1½ cups cream, whipped
2 cups fresh strawberries, sliced
Additional powdered sugar (optional)

For the crepe batter:
Place all the ingredients in a blender. Blend until smooth.

Lightly grease a nonstick crepe pan or frying pan. Heat to medium heat. Pour ¼ cup of batter into a small puddle in the center of the pan. Holding the handle, tilt the pan in a circular motion to allow the batter to evenly coat the bottom of the pan in a thin layer.

Cook until tiny bubbles form in the center and the edges begin to curl. Flip and cook the other side until lightly brown. Place on a plate and repeat with remaining batter. Stack the crepes on top of each other, keeping them warm by covering them with a towel or an inverted plate.

For the filling:
Beat cream cheese until smooth. Add powdered sugar and vanilla. Beat. Fold in the whipped cream.

Spread a generous layer of the cream filling down the center of each crepe. Top with sliced strawberries and roll tightly.

To serve, place a dollop of cream and a few strawberries on top of the rolled crepes and/or sprinkle with powdered sugar.

Yields approximately 12 crepes.

*To make gluten-free crepes, simply substitute the flour for a good quality GF all-purpose flour. Be sure that the blend includes xanthan gum.

Tip: Substitute strawberries with another of your favorite fruits, such as blueberries, raspberries, or sliced peaches. Alternatively, if you prefer Bram's flavor of choice, spread the crepe with a thin layer of Nutella and roll.

Rosamund and Alice noticed Gwen's new scarf and mittens as soon as they saw her, and when they asked about them, Gwen admitted they were a birthday gift. The girls then insisted that they stop at the local shop at the end of the day, where they pooled their money to buy Gwen a few pieces of treacle toffee. By the time she went to bed that night, Gwen determined that it had been the best day she'd experienced since she'd moved to Llanfyllin.

One Last Spring
Sian Ann Bessey

Treacle Toffee

3 ounces molasses
3 ounces golden syrup*
A rounded ¾ cup brown sugar
3 tablespoons butter
¼ teaspoon cream of tartar

*If you are unable to find golden syrup, corn syrup may be used.

Line an 8-inch square pan with parchment paper.

Place all the ingredients in a thick-bottomed saucepan. Warm over medium heat until butter has melted. Increase heat and stir continually until mixture comes to a full rolling boil. When the mixture reaches 285°F on a candy thermometer, pour into the lined pan.

If you want even pieces, wait until the toffee is cool enough to handle, but soft enough that a finger pressed in the top leaves a slight indentation. Score the toffee into squares with an oiled knife. When the toffee has cooled completely, break along the lines.

For a more traditional, old-fashioned approach, wait until the toffee has cooled completely, then break it into shards with a rolling pin.

Store in an airtight container with a piece of parchment paper between each layer to prevent the pieces from sticking together.

Yields 64 one-inch square pieces.

Tip: If you do not have a candy thermometer, drizzle a small amount of the mixture into a cup of cold water. You will know when the mixture is ready because it will be firm to the touch rather than soft.

Every time Prince Garrett moved to take a bite, someone else would ask him a question.

As Janessa ate her dessert, something sinfully chocolate and airy, her sympathies went out to the prince. He never even got a chance to pick up his spoon.

Royal Target
Traci Hunter Abramson

Chocolate Mousse

Mousse:
3 tablespoons unsalted butter
1 cup semi-sweet chocolate chips
1¼ cup heavy whipping cream
2 tablespoons sugar

Whipped cream:
½ cup heavy whipping cream
2 teaspoons sugar

For the mousse:
Before beginning, put large mixing bowl and beaters in freezer for at least 10 minutes. Chill an additional bowl in freezer or refrigerator.

Place butter and chocolate chips in a microwave-safe bowl. Microwave for thirty seconds. Stir. Microwave for another 15–20 seconds until melted. Set aside.

In the first chilled bowl, whip 1¼ cups whipping cream with electric mixer until soft peaks begin to form. Add 2 tablespoons sugar gradually. Continue beating until peaks begin to stiffen.

Pour melted chocolate into the other chilled bowl. Fold in ⅓ of whipped cream mixture. Mix gently until well blended. Repeat the process with another third of the whipped cream, and again with the last third. Spoon mousse equally into 12 small serving dishes and chill for at least 4 hours.

For the whipped cream:
Whip ½ cup heavy whipping cream until soft peaks form. Add 2 teaspoons sugar and continue whipping until desired texture. Spoon on top of mousse. Serve cold.

Yields 12 servings.

This no-fail pastry recipe is good enough to serve to those who don't need to eat gluten-free, but those with allergies will love you forever if you use it to make a delicious pie.

Sian Ann Bessey

Gluten-Free Pastry

⅓ cup cold water
2 teaspoons apple cider vinegar
2 egg yolks, beaten
1 cup rice flour
1 cup cornstarch
½ cup tapioca starch
2 teaspoons xanthan gum
¼ teaspoon salt
½ cup shortening
½ cup cold butter, grated*

In a small bowl, combine cold water, vinegar, and egg yolks. Set aside.

In a large bowl, sift rice flour, cornstarch, tapioca starch, xanthan gum, and salt. Using a pastry blender or two knives, cut in shortening and butter until mixture resembles small peas. Stirring with a fork, pour egg yolk mixture, a little at a time, over the flour mixture to make soft dough.

Divide dough in half. Gently form the dough into two balls and place each one on plastic wrap. Flatten into a disk and wrap well. Refrigerate for at least 1 hour. Let cold pastry stand for 10 minutes at room temperature before rolling out.

Preheat oven to 425°F.

Place the pastry disk between two sheets of waxed paper. Gently roll out the pastry dough into a circle 1 inch larger than the diameter of the pie plate. Remove the top sheet of waxed paper. Invert the pastry over the pie plate, easing it in. Carefully remove the remaining sheet of waxed paper.

Trim excess pastry to edge of pie plate and patch any cracks with trimmings. If baking unfilled pastry shell, prick bottom and sides with fork. Bake for 15–20 minutes or until golden. To bake filled pastry shell, do not prick. Fill and top with a second sheet of pastry. Seal and crimp edges. Cut half a dozen ½-inch slits in the top crust. Bake according to individual recipe directions.

*The ½ cup butter can be replaced by ½ cup shortening (1 cup total) to make the pastry dairy-free.

Yields 1 double-crust or 2 single-crust pies.

From Sian Ann Bessey's Kitchen

Bean Salsa
Honey-Roasted Nuts
Apple Cider
Woodcroft Hall's Drinking Chocolate
Mrs. Nesbitt's Griddlecakes
The Duke of Kelbrook's Chelsea Buns
Mair's Bara Brith
Spiced Buns
Artisan Bread
Quick and Easy Wheat Bread
Mrs. Nesbitt's Oat Bread
Gluten-Free Cornbread
Cheesy Potato and Leek Soup
Welsh Cawl
Butternut Squash Soup
Potato Salad
Christmas Market Kartoffelpuffer
Cheesy Dill Au Gratin Potatoes
Welsh Mint Sauce
Hungarian Goulash
Cornish Pasties
Deadline-Crunch Cashew Pad Thai
Should Have Chosen Chicken Tikka Masala
Spent-All-Day-Writing Chicken Tetrazzini
Mrs. Miller's Macaroni and Cheese
Welsh Cakes
Victoria Sandwich
Finley Park's Orange Blossom Cake
Cheesecake
Chocolate Cheesecake
Dorcas's Apple Pie
Traditional English Mince Pies
Finley Park Cream Puffs
Christmas Market Gingerbread Men
Lord Dunsbourne's Oatmeal Biscuits
Sugar Cookies
Katy's Brownies
Good-Enough-to-Have-for-Dinner Donuts
Dessert Crepes
Treacle Toffee
Gluten-Free Pastry

From Sarah M. Eden's Kitchen

Raspberry Shrub
Dairy-Free, Egg-Free, Nut-Free 6-Week Breakfast Muffins
Scones
Clotted Cream
Katie's Irish Soda Bread
Clover Rolls
Ham and Lentil Stew
Potato Stew
Bean Soup
Spinach, Tomato, and Chicken Pasta Salad
Colcannon
Oven-Roasted Vegetables
Raisin Sauce for Ham
Easy Hand Pies
Dublin Coddle
Mock Chicken Alfredo
Ratatouille
Layton and Caroline's Twelfth Night Cake
Fairy Cakes
Strawberry Pie
Fruit Tart
Bread Pudding
Cardamom Shortbread
Mater's Ginger Biscuits
Lucas's Peppermint Ice Cream

From Traci Hunter Abramson's Kitchen

Potato Bites
Crab-Stuffed Mushrooms
Saint Squad Sliders
Peanut Butter Smoothie
Strawberry-Banana Smoothie
Traci's Survival Smoothie
Mushroom Quiche
Patrice's Quiche Florentine
Eggs Benedict
Jocelyn's Scrambled Eggs
Blueberry Muffins
Streusel Muffins
Katherine's Cinnamon Rolls

Irresistible Banana Bread
Cornbread
Simple Dinner Rolls
Maya's Indian Flatbread (Naan)
Clam Chowder
Cheddar Chowder
Nolan's Cream of Mushroom Soup
Pea Soup
It-Won't-Kill-Me Salad
Broccoli Salad
Shrimp Pasta Salad
CJ's Chicken Salad
Rice with Caramelized Onions
Garlic Mashed Potatoes
Charlotte's Flank Steak
Steak Diane
Pot Roast
Even-Amy-Can-Make-It Meatloaf
Grilled Beef and Scallop Kabobs
Catalina Pork Chops
Curry Chicken
Charlie's Southwestern Chicken and Rice
Irresistible Chicken Enchiladas
Cas's Chicken Crepes
Chicken Cordon Bleu
Chicken Parmesan
Apricot-Glazed Salmon
Arepas con Queso
Where's Kade's Pizza?
Riley's Lasagna
Simply Special Stroganoff
Shaye's Tuna Casserole
Cherry Cobbler
Baklava
Miss Carol's Chocolate Chip Cookies
Mint Brownies
Chocolate Mousse

Index

OTHER BOOKS AND AUDIOBOOKS BY SARAH M. EDEN

The Lancaster Family

Seeking Persephone

Courting Miss Lancaster

Romancing Daphne

Loving Lieutenant Lancaster

Christmas at Falstone Castle
in *All Hearts Come Home for Christmas* anthology

Charming Artemis

The Gents

Forget Me Not

Lily of the Valley

Fleur de Lis
(Coming June 2023)

The Huntresses

The Best-Laid Plans

The Best Intentions

The Jonquil Brothers

The Kiss of a Stranger

Friends and Foes

Drops of Gold

As You Are

A Fine Gentleman

For Love or Honor

The Heart of a Vicar

Charming Artemis

Stand-alones

Glimmer of Hope

An Unlikely Match

For Elise

CHRONOLOGICAL ORDER OF ALL RELATED SARAH M. EDEN GEORGIAN- & REGENCY-ERA BOOKS

Forget Me Not
Lily of the Valley
Fleur de Lis
Seeking Persephone
Courting Miss Lancaster
Glimmer of Hope
Romancing Daphne
The Kiss of a Stranger
Friends and Foes
Drops of Gold
For Elise
As You Are
A Fine Gentleman
For Love or Honor
Loving Lieutenant Lancaster
Christmas at Falstone Castle
The Heart of a Vicar
The Best-Laid Plans
Charming Artemis
The Best Intentions

© Melea Nelson 2021

Sarah M. Eden is a *USA Today* best-selling author of witty and charming historical romances, including 2020's *Foreword Reviews* INDIE Awards Gold winner for romance, *Forget Me Not*, 2019's *Foreword Reviews* INDIE Awards Gold winner for romance, *The Lady and the Highwayman*, and 2020 Holt Medallion finalist, *Healing Hearts*. She is a two-time Best of State Gold Medal winner for fiction and a three-time Whitney Award winner. Combining her obsession with history and her affinity for tender love stories, Sarah loves crafting deep characters and heartfelt romances set against rich historical backdrops. She holds a bachelor's degree in research and happily spends hours perusing the reference shelves of her local library.

www.SarahMEden.com

OTHER BOOKS AND AUDIOBOOKS BY SIAN ANN BESSEY

Georgian Gentlemen Series

The Noble Smuggler

An Uncommon Earl

An Alleged Rogue

An Unfamiliar Duke

The Unassuming Curator
(Coming April 2023)

Contemporary

Forgotten Notes

Cover of Darkness

Deception

You Came for Me

The Insider

The Gem Thief

Historical

Within the Dark Hills

One Last Spring

To Win a Lady's Heart

For Castle and Crown

The Heart of the Rebellion

The Call of the Sea

Falcon Point Series

Heirs of Falcon Point

The Danger with Diamonds

Kids on a Mission Series

Escape from Germany

Uprising in Samoa

Ambushed in Africa

Children's

A Family Is Forever

Teddy Bear, Blankie, and a Prayer

Anthologies and Booklets

The Perfect Gift

A Hopeful Christmas

No Strangers at Christmas

© Melea Nelson 2021

Sian Ann Bessey was born in Cambridge, England, and grew up on the island of Anglesey off the coast of North Wales. She left her homeland to attend university in the U.S., where she earned a bachelor's degree in communications, with a minor in English.

She began her writing career as a student, publishing several articles in magazines while still in college. Since then, she has published historical romance and romantic suspense novels, along with a variety of children's books. She is a *USA Today* best-selling author, a Foreword Reviews Book of the Year finalist, and a Whitney Award finalist.

Sian and her husband, Kent, are the parents of five children and the grandparents of three beautiful girls and two handsome boys. They currently live in Southeast Idaho, and although Sian doesn't have the opportunity to speak Welsh very often anymore, Llanfairpwllgwyngyllgogerychwyrndrobwllllantysiliogogogoch still rolls off her tongue.

Traveling, reading, cooking, and being with her grandchildren are some of Sian's favorite activities. She also loves hearing from her readers. If you would like to contact her, she can be reached through her website at www.siananbessey.com, her Facebook group, Author Sian Ann Bessey's Corner, and on Instagram, @sian_bessey.

OTHER BOOKS AND AUDIO PRODUCTS BY TRACI HUNTER ABRAMSON

UNDERCURRENTS SERIES

Undercurrents

Ripple Effect

The Deep End

SAINT SQUAD SERIES

Freefall

Lockdown

Crossfire

Backlash

Smoke Screen

Code Word

Lock and Key

Drop Zone

Spotlight

Tripwire

Redemption

Covert Ops
(Coming May 2023)

ROYAL SERIES

Royal Target

Royal Secrets

Royal Brides

Royal Heir

GUARDIAN SERIES

Failsafe

Safe House

Sanctuary

On the Run

In Harm's Way

Not Dead Yet

Unseen
(Coming August 2023)

DREAM'S EDGE SERIES

*Dancing to Freedom**

An Unlikely Pair

*Broken Dreams**

Dreams of Gold

*The Best Mistake**

Worlds Collide

FALCON POINT SERIES

Heirs of Falcon Point

The Danger with Diamonds

STAND-ALONES

Obsession

Proximity

*Entangled**

*Twisted Fate**

*Sinister Secrets**

Deep Cover

Mistaken Reality

Kept Secrets

Chances Are

Chance for Home

A Change of Fortune

*Novella

© Melea Nelson 2021

Traci Hunter Abramson was born in Arizona, where she lived until moving to Venezuela for a study-abroad program. After graduating from Brigham Young University, she worked for the Central Intelligence Agency, eventually resigning in order to raise her family. She credits the CIA with giving her a wealth of ideas as well as the skills needed to survive her children's teenage years. She loves to travel and recently retired after spending twenty-six years coaching her local high school swim team. She has written more than forty best-selling novels and is a seven-time Whitney Award winner, including 2017 and 2019 Best Novel of the Year.

She also loves hearing from her readers. If you would like to contact her, she can be reached through the following:

www.traciabramson.com
Facebook group: Traci's Friends
bookbub.com/authors/traci-hunter-abramson
twitter@traciabramson
facebook.com/tracihabramson
instagram.com/traciabramson.com